THIN

Catching up to Anorexia

by Shawn Willson M.D.

DORRANCE PUBLISHING CO
EST. 1920
PITTSBURGH, PENNSYLVANIA 15238

Dorrance Publishing Co
585 Alpha Drive
Suite 103
Pittsburgh, PA 15238
Visit our website at *www.dorrancebookstore.com*

ISBN: 979-8-89211-227-7
eISBN: 979-8-89211-725-8

CHAPTER 1

THIN

"Great minds have purposes, others just have wishes."
- Washington Irving

I was at a hospital fundraiser for diabetes. It was about 2:30 in the afternoon. It was Saint Joseph Medical Center, where I was a psychiatric consultant. I was chit chatting with some of my favorite physicians when one of my friends, who was in charge of the fundraising, came up to me and first asked how I was doing. It was Amy Manske, Molly Manske's mom, someone my daughter McKenzie played softball with.

After a few other party-like questions she said, very directly "Shawn, have you seen your daughter lately?"

I stared at her! I had no idea what she was talking about, but she had such a serious look on her face I knew I'd better listen.

There was silence until I finally asked her, "What do you mean?"

And she said, "She is so thin."

Thin! Thin! My heart stopped and my thoughts started racing. Have I noticed any weight changes in McKenzie lately? Had I not been watching my own daughter? The tone of Amy's voice scared me. It then came to me. Because I am a psychiatrist, I knew exactly what she meant by "thin". I had heard the word "thin" so many times in my practice that I knew what it really meant. Could my daughter possibly have anorexia? I was scared and didn't feel like talking anymore. So I tossed my plastic cup of cheap chardonnay into the trash and ran for the car. Somehow, I made it without tripping. I got in the car, buckled up, turned on the ignition, pressed down on the gas, and headed straight for Indian Hills Junior High School.

My daughter lived with me. It had always been just her and I. Her dad had been involved until she was three when we moved from Colorado to New Hampshire. That was so I could do my fellowship in forensics at Dartmouth. I thought we were pretty close, had I not been looking? As I was driving my mind was rushing through some of the thin patients I had seen on the Research Eating Disorder Unit when covering for my partner. The first one I thought of was Chrissy, a tall blonde, probably 5'8", who wore a size 2 in clothes. I pictured her running down the hallway yelling "Dr. Willson, Dr. Willson, I am so fat." Or Julie who was 5'5" weighing in at eighty-seven pounds who I found under one of those tall hospital beds doing crunches. Of course there was no exercise allowed while on the unit, only eating. Eat, eat, and then eat some more.

As I pulled up to Indian Hills, I spotted my daughter amongst the other students walking across the grass, heading home. She was thin! I could see it now from a mile away. So, why couldn't I see it when it was right in front of me? This was a question I asked myself many times since that day.

McKenzie was thirteen years old at the time. She was 5'4½" tall, had brown hair that was bobbed, big brown eyes, and a smile you don't forget. She was beautiful. I'm a psychiatrist. I have been a psychiatrist for over twenty-five years with an education from Dartmouth, Emory, and Harvard. Anorexia was in my scope of practice and yet I still missed it? It wasn't even on my radar. But it should have been. The statistics fit my daughter: A thirteen-year-old female who was starting to diet. This early stage is what I will call possible anorexia. Anorexia usually occurs in young girls from ages twelve to eighteen. I should've been looking for it, but I wasn't. McKenzie saw my car and climbed in.

I remained silent and started the drive home. I felt speechless at first. I wanted to keep staring at her.

Finally, I composed myself and said as calmly as possible, "McKenzie, you're so thin. What has happened?"

She quickly said back, "No, I'm not thin, Mom."

I said, "Have you looked at yourself in the mirror?"

McKenzie has told me since that day that at first she did think she was fat. But later knew she was actually thin and liked it.

"No, I don't want to see a fat girl."

She turned her head towards the window and refused to talk to me the rest of the way home. I begged her to. I was desperate for answers. But we ended up driving home in silence.

Once home, she ran up the stairs saying she was going to do homework.

I said, "It's Friday."

She said, "I don't care."

I knew then we had a problem.

McKenzie always talks to me about what happens at school but she was stone-cold silent.

After she went upstairs, I sat down in my big, red Lazy-Boy chair and began to think really deeply. At the end of every day since that day I would long to be in my big red chair. It became my refuge.

I wracked my brain for any clues of when all this might've started. I first thought there was nothing to indicate anorexia. Maybe it's something else like a stomach parasite or some other disease. But I knew that was ridiculous, and suddenly, I did remember something. A few months ago, McKenzie had come home from school saying a boy in her class had repeatedly asked her what her weight was, obviously implying that she was that fat. He was a bully and he got to my kid. I, of course, was angry at the time but didn't know what to do. I felt helpless as she repeatedly, day after day, asked me if it was true. I told her she was beautiful and that she wasn't fat. She finally stopped asking me, so I thought she had gotten over it. Boy, I guess I was wrong.

I later found out that McKenzie had gone to see the counselor for help with this issue but was number twenty-seven in line. Twenty-seven! This was so disheartening. So I guess none of us parents can expect the school to watch for problems like anorexia, anxiety, drugs, and depression. Number twenty-seven was not going to work. We, as a community of parents, need to be watching out for our kids. As you will learn later, Molly Manske's mom saved McKenzie's life. She was the only one of the other mothers who noticed or maybe who had the courage to say something to me. Some people might say other people's children are not our business, but I disagree, it is more than just a business to take care of each other's kids. I believe it is our duty.

After sitting in my chair for at least an hour just thinking about how thin McKenzie looked, I decided to go upstairs and try to talk to her one more time.

I stood at the top of the stairs and looked in her room. I cautiously said, "Can we talk? I would actually like to weigh you." I knew she had a scale in her bedroom.

She quickly got up from her bed and slammed the door shut. "I don't want to talk," she yelled through the door.

But I kept talking. "Are you coming down for dinner?"

She opened her door and yelled, "No!"

I got another glimpse at her and immediately thought that she didn't look like my McKenzie, she was too thin.

I babbled, "I know I don't get home most nights until seven, but I always brought home something to eat. I thought you were eating up in your room, that's why I didn't see food downstairs. But now I know you weren't even eating, were you?"

She screamed again, "I don't want to talk to you!"

This behavior was so reactive and out of line with my well-behaved gentle daughter. It was alarming. Her irritability would soon be a regular occurrence from here on out with every discussion we would have about weight or food. I left her alone and went back downstairs. I made myself a peanut butter and jelly sandwich. I sat in my big red chair until I fell asleep.

The next day, Saturday, was the day before Mother's Day. McKenzie left to go to a friend's house where she stayed all day and evening. I had a party to go to that night so we had very little discussion at all. Once we were both at home, I knew I wouldn't get anywhere bringing up weight again. While at the party, I walked around like a zombie. I know now that this is what trauma feels like. Fight, flight, or freeze. I was freezing. I was so anxious. I could not get the vision of her being so thin out of my head. I was yelling inside but, speechless on the outside. My mind couldn't stop spinning. I knew that anorexia was so dangerous. The most dangerous mental illness. I finally left and cried all the way home. Back to the red chair.

I wanted to call someone, but who? Friends? Family? At that time I was foolishly very proud. I was ashamed of myself, as well as McKenzie. Or was it guilt? Probably both. I didn't call anyone. In retrospect, I wasn't as close to my daughter as I thought. I loved her like no other love but where did I spend my time? I now see how she could have benefited from more time with me. I had to admit to myself I had been really consumed with my practice. It was still very new and growing. It was actually a clinic that I called the Purple Door. I was very driven. I was driven even with my tennis game. I had to play every night. I had been blind. I got up out of the chair, grabbed my rackets and threw them away.

The next morning I woke up realizing it was Mother's Day. And then it really hit me. Instead of it being a joyful day, it was painful. A day that I can now see like it was yesterday. My daughter was in trouble and we needed a plan. Where to go first? Do I take her to the emergency room? Do I have a family intervention? I knew she would not comply with either of these plans. For some reason, I didn't think about the eating disorder (ED) unit at that time, but I did come up with a "creative" plan. I thought I could possibly persuade her, so I headed upstairs.

I was hoping to find her in a good mood. I found her rummaging around in her room.

When she saw me she said in a very chipper voice, "Good morning, Mom! Happy Mother's Day. I have a card for you."

She handed me this really big card which was homemade, my favorite. It was the kind of card all of us mothers like best. Inside it said, "Thanks Mom, for always being there for me." Inside the card listed all the reasons she loved me. I cried of course. Tears came running down my face. So many mixed emotions were already so bottled up. I took the Kleenex my daughter handed me, wiped my face, smiled, and said thank you.

I must have said thank you to her at least a hundred more times. McKenzie reached out to hug me, and as I wrapped my arms around her, I felt her small frame; she had lost so much weight.

I softly said, "We have to talk McKenzie."

To my surprise, she sat down.

I sat down next to her. I had this creative plan I thought might work so went on to say, "You and I are both concerned about your weight for different reasons." She was silent so I went on, "I think we should see a nutritionist that I know. Her name is Katie, I know her from the eating disorder unit at research medical center. If you're going to try to lose weight, you at least need to do it in a healthy way."

Miraculously, she said, "Okay."

I didn't waste any time. I went downstairs and called Katie.

Even though it was Mother's Day, I took my chance and called her. I felt bad for calling her on a holiday. But finally decided it was the right thing to do. Thankfully, she answered the phone. I felt desperate. I told her how thin McKenzie looked. And how she was refusing to eat. She kindly said she would see us during her lunch break the next day and to be at her office around 12 p.m. I had to make a decision of what to do with my patients the next day. I can't think of the last time I was unable to be in the office but, this felt so overwhelming I didn't think I had a choice. I texted my office manager, who was my aunt, and told her to clear my time from 11-2 the next day.

CHAPTER 2

THE NUTRITIONIST

"To eat bread without hope is still slowly to starve to death."
- Pearl S. Buck

The next morning, we got up. I had breakfast. McKenzie refused without even the slightest consideration. I had an English muffin with peanut butter. I really love my peanut butter. No need to fight, we were pursuing an answer. I told Mckenzie I would pick her up at 11:30 and then head to Katie's office. Once I got to work and walked in the door, I saw one of my favorite patients. She looked at me with eager eyes and said she really needed to talk to me. So I was somehow able to put on my white jacket and get to work helping others.

I loved my patients. I always felt like it was an honor to help them. The morning went fast and at 11:15 I headed to the school to get McKenzie. I picked her up and we headed for Katie's office. I tried to make small talk by asking her if she was enjoying her teachers and if she liked PE. And she answered me politely, but didn't offer any spontaneous conversation back. We were both nervous. Once in Katie's office, we were sitting on these stiff orange chairs. Both of us were pretending to read magazines. I found myself listlessly paging through a *Sports Illustrated* that had Serena Williams on the front.

I always liked Katie. She was sweet and thorough with the patients, but right now I was really nervous about what might be said between McKenzie and I. My neck felt tight. I kept shaking my right leg. I could tell by the way she was sitting, real close to the edge of the chair, that McKenzie was nervous as well.

What were we heading in for here on this Monday morning? I continued to make small talk but without much success. Did I even have a good relationship with my daughter? Had I been missing out this whole time? Then Katie rescued us. Once inside her office, we sat apart on two overstuffed chairs. Katie sat behind her desk. She introduced herself and told McKenzie some of the things a nutritionist does. She said they advise clients on their food choices and the impact it has on one's health. She then asked McKenzie what she would like from this appointment.

McKenzie said, "I don't know."

There was a silence, then Katie kindly said, "The first thing we need to record is your weight. May we start with weighing you?"

McKenzie agreed and stepped up on the scale.

Katie looked at me and said "Ninety-five pounds."

My heart sank. I froze. I couldn't speak. She should be weighing at least 115 lbs.

Twenty pounds underweight. What is happening? I am freaking out inside. I couldn't help it. I started crying.

Katie took a moment then said, "McKenzie, do you see that you are underweight?

McKenzie said, "No."

Katie then said, "On a scale of zero to ten, how motivated are you to gain weight?"

McKenzie said, "Zero."

I couldn't believe what I was hearing.

Katie then said, "Mom, how motivated are you for McKenzie to gain weight?"

I blurted out, "Ten." Katie didn't say anything but I did. "McKenzie we are heading to the hospital."

Katie then got out her calculator, put in some numbers, then looked up and said McKenzie's BMI (Body Mass Index) is 15.8. A healthy BMI is 18.5 or greater. She was in trouble and I knew it. The numbers were all pointing in the same direction, trouble. We needed more than Katie. There was not really anything else to say. It was time to take the next step.

So I said, "McKenzie let's go, we are headed to the Research Medical Center where there is an eating disorder unit."

Katie's silence gave me the support I needed. I knew she agreed, but then there was McKenzie shaking her head, no. What kind of mom was I to let her get into this condition? I realized I did not have time to feel sorry for myself. We had to move with this new plan.

I looked at Katie and said, "There's a problem; do you agree?"

She looked at McKenzie, then at me, and said, "Yes."

We used to use the BMI to gauge the severity of weight loss but now we lean more toward someone's ideal weight. A BMI is calculated by weight or pounds divided by height in inches squared, multiplied by 703. A BMI below 18.5 is low. 18.5-24.9 is a healthy BMI. A 5'5" tall female should weigh 114-144. The new school of thought around weight determination is to use ideal body weight by dividing one's BMI by what is a normal BMI to get the percentage of ideal body weight. So, McKenzie was at 83% Ideal Body Weight. When someone is 70%-84% of IBW, they are best served at the nearest inpatient facility. With an 85%-94% IBW, then outpatient programs are usually sufficient.

I grabbed McKenzie's hand, and said, "What is happening with you, honey?"

She said, "Mom, leave me alone. You don't understand."

I knew I couldn't argue with her now. People with anorexia get their strength and self-esteem by not eating. It also gives them a sense of relief from emotional stress. They are often very irrational and resistant to any suggestions. I knew that McKenzie would not want to go in-patient, but we had to do it. McKenzie's life depended on getting treatment. I had concocted a plan to work around her resistance: I was going to get her into the car by saying we had to go home, and then once in the car, we'd go to the gas station where I could have a friend come meet me and help me get McKenzie to the hospital.

So, I said, "McKenzie, let's go home."

She agreed.

I thanked Katie, and we were off. Once in the car I casually mentioned, "McKenzie, I need gas."

She again said, "Okay."

We headed for QuikTrip, where I always go for gas, so I can get my coffee that I like. We pulled in.

After filling up the car with gas, I got in the car and without looking at her I said, "McKenzie, we have to go to the hospital."

McKenzie immediately whipped open the car door and started running. I couldn't tell where she was going, but she didn't go into the QuikTrip. I sat in my car for about ten minutes, when I saw her circling back around and going into QuikTrip, probably to hide in the bathroom. I jumped out and called out to my daughter.

At this point, we had things stirred up at the gas station with a little bit of an audience with McKenzie yelling at me, "I want to go home!"

Meanwhile, I had called two friends to ask for help, but neither one of them were home. And then I thought that I could call my mom. McKenzie loved my mom; maybe she could help. I punched in her number and thank God, she answered. I told her about the situation. She said she'd be here in ten minutes. I went into QuikTrip to find McKenzie, who was likely in the bathroom. Sure enough, I found her in one of the bathroom stalls. I asked her to please come out, and she said no. What could I do now? I went back out of the bathroom and noticed people staring at me. This is not how I want to get attention in my life. I decided to go outside and wait in the car for my mom.

A few minutes later, I saw mom's navy blue Lexus coming down the road. She pulled in and parked in a quiet manner in a space near the QuikTrip building. I already felt better. I went inside and told McKenzie that her grandmother was here to see her. McKenzie pushed past me and out the door and got in Mom's car. It seemed like forever, but it was about fifteen minutes later when my mom rolled down her window and told me to come over to the car.

Once I got there, she simply said, "I think we're ready to go to the hospital."

McKenzie said nothing.

I said, "Okay, follow me."

We caravanned to the Research Medical Center which had the only eating disorder unit in the region. Luckily the eating disorder unit at Research was a good one.

I was getting my team together. Now, not only did I have Katie on my team, but also my mom. You need everyone you can get. I realized almost too late that you cannot do this alone, so it's definitely important to shore up a support team as fast as possible.

To this day, I don't know what my mom really said to McKenzie to convince her to go to the hospital.

I asked her, but she said, "We just talked about school."

I said, "Are you kidding?"

I did make one observation that I now know could have made a difference that day. Mom gave McKenzie the biggest hug when she got into the car. People with an eating disorder have a lot of nervous energy, making them very uncomfortable. Touching means a lot. It calms them down, something my daughter would confirm with me later.

As we headed to Research Medical Center, I made a call to the unit to tell them we were coming only to find out through the recording that it was closed. Closed! What were we going to do? This couldn't be happening. I quickly called the emergency room to find out who the "hospitalist" was for the day. This was the doctor on call who did all the hospital in-patient admissions. I found out it was my friend Ellen. I was so relieved, maybe she could help. About this time, we were rolling into the parking lot of Research, and as I was waiting on a callback, I told McKenzie to sit tight.

Ellen got back to me right away. She confirmed that the unit was closed. She said that it didn't have any patients.

I said, "You do now."

There was a silence on the other end of the phone then she said, "Agreed."

She told me to meet her at the unit in twenty minutes. Ellen was now on the team with Katie and Mom. Hopefully I would get more on my team when at Research. The nurses and the counselors there made the unit what it was. I remember them working with me as a psychiatrist, they were always very pro-fessional. It takes a special person to work with someone who has an eating disorder because they are so resistant to getting better. The nurses and coun-selors were seasoned. I was already counting on them.

Twenty minutes later, McKenzie and I were waiting for the elevator to take us to the fourth floor where the eating disorder unit resided. I had been there so many times to see patients and now it was my daughter. When I pushed the elevator button, my blood became electric. I felt frozen. This was not my girl. It couldn't be happening. I wanted to run away and act as if none of this was happening, but I somehow looked at my skinny little girl and smiled. I kept seeing her as that cute little kindergartner with a pixie haircut who wore the same dress to kindergarten every day. Sweet.

When the elevator door opened, Ellen was there waiting for us in her crisp white jacket. I wanted to hug her but decided on the professional pose. I introduced Ellen to McKenzie. Ellen said to follow her to the examination room. I was to stay behind. This was it; my McKenzie was being admitted into the eating disorder unit. They turned and walked down the hall. Somehow, I got back on the elevator, pressed the button for the first-floor cafeteria, and as the doors shut, I crouched down and wept.

We were in trouble and we were very late in the game. We need to catch these girls at the earlier stage which I will call possible anorexia. We need to start talking out loud about it. It is here to stay. Some of these girls that are dieting finally decide why not just starve? Thinking that taking control of eating will control everything. Eating disorders are a common occurrence, not a problem to hide in the closet. Fifty percent of people know someone with an eating disorder. If you can identify someone with symptoms or signs of a possible eating disorder, let the parent or teacher know.

CHAPTER 3

POSSIBLE ANOREXIA

"Having a goal is a state of happiness."
- E.J. Bartek

So what is anorexia? It is defined in the Diagnostic Statistical Manual of Mental Disorders as being a disease with the following criteria: A significantly low weight that is less than minimally normal, an intense fear of becoming fat even though at a significantly low weight, and a disturbance in the way one looks at their body. Basically, it is someone at a significantly low weight who continues to starve themselves with a fear of gaining weight or being fat. According to the National Eating Disorder Association, there is a new concern about someone who drops weight way too fast while starving themself. The significant drop in weight, even if someone is overweight, is of concern too because they become malnourished. Malnourishment is the main concern for any of the eating disorders.

There is a term I would like to use when we talk about early signs of anorexia, called "possible anorexia". Research shows that if you get someone in the possible anorexia stage that there is a ninety-five percent chance of recovery. We as a community need to keep our eyes open for these kids because there are more now than ever. In this book we focus on young girls ages twelve to eighteen for this is the age with the highest risk, but the risk of boys getting it has also doubled. The rate of anorexia in boys is one percent.

The overall rate of anorexia has doubled since the Covid-19 pandemic. The prevalence of possible anorexia is 7.4% of the population. There is a thirty-nine percent higher chance of a teen getting anorexia since Covid-19. This is likely due to all the isolation leading to more social media which leads to more self consciousness. These days teens are all alone. Picture them, each one, alone in their bed each night with the scary world in front of them, with pictures of perfect, beautiful people on social media. People usually look their best on social media. This can be intimidating.

There is a new thought trying to explain anorexia. The thinking seems to be similar to the extremist. For example, individuals who are ultramarathoners or those who climb the tallest mountains. I can see that in my daughter. She certainly was disciplined and living on the edge.

The mortality rate from malnourishment or suicide from anorexia is six times greater than average within girls ages twelve to eighteen. It has the highest mortality rate of any psychiatric disorder.

How often do we talk about anorexia? Never? So how often should we be talking about anorexia? All the time.

If only one out of ten girls with anorexia ever seek help, where are the other nine? We are not looking for anorexia because it's associated with a lot of shame. Unfortunately, families are left alone desperately struggling to keep their loved ones alive. Here's the thing, if we can detour a young girl from gaining any momentum with anorexia we can prevent those neural pathways from laying down.

Once they have laid down patterns of thinking, it becomes like a rut in the muddy road that's very hard to get out of. It's called neuroplasticity. The more we think or do something the easier it is the next time. For some reason this really applies to anorexia.

So, these young girls are dying from malnourishment, starving themselves, and what do we do? Where do we start? We start by looking at young girls' eating habits. I'm going to give you a list of signs to look for in your children, or in other children. It is actually really exciting. By talking about it out loud, we will identify it quicker and seek the appropriate treatment right away. We thus save these families from great pain.

The following are signs of possible anorexia:

- Small portions of food

- Talking about food all the time
- Not wanting to eat around others
- Excessive exercise
- Complaining of being full all the time
- Rituals with food or unusual eating behavior
- Skipping meals
- Isolation
- Fixation on meal preparation
- Dramatic weight loss
- Dressing with layers of clothes so others will not see their weight loss. Plus they also need to stay warm. Anorexia is associated with a much lower body temperature
- Refusing certain food groups
- Talking about the need for fewer calories
- Denying being hungry
- Strong need to control
- A restriction of emotions

I know not all of these directly involve food but behavior is just as important. Thanks to technology, we have two apps that will also help us uncover anorexia. One is Rise Up and Recover, and the other is the Eating Disorder Test. Both have a helpline associated with them.

Of course there is also the National Eating Disorder Association that lists support groups all over the United States. Now with technology, you can join these meetings from the comfort of your family room.

So what happens if you notice these behaviors? For example, if you observe your daughter's friend picking at their food every time they are over you can say to the parent, "Have you noticed any changes in your daughter's eating habits?" Or if you notice significant weight loss say to the parent, "It looks like your daughter has lost a lot of weight."

Now for parents already involved in possible anorexia or anorexia. The point is not to control, judge, or punish these young people who have this disorder. The point is to set boundaries and to maintain a position of gentle, but clear authority with the help of a physician or counselor.

Here's a case study to emphasize the concept of boundaries. Rosie was sixteen when she first was seen for treatment. Her parents said she had recently lost eighteen pounds which changed her appearance from a toned athlete to an emaciated victim of starvation. Despite the rapid weight loss, she remained a straight-A student, plus she was captain of the high school basketball team.

Once Rosie's parents had noticed how much weight she had lost they took her to their physician who helped them to set up boundaries. They determined an ideal weight for her if she was to avoid a higher level of care. She was to gain one to two pounds a week if she wanted to continue playing basketball. This was even though her team was ranked high and planning on going to finals.

Rosie was furious and her parents were scared which often occurs when boundaries are set. They also found a family therapist who specialized in eating disorders for more support. The parents were told to eat every breakfast and dinner with their daughter.

The basketball finals were in two weeks. Rosie would have to gain two pounds to attend. The first week she continued to refuse to eat and even lost half a pound. The next week started out the same but Rosie's parents made it clear they meant business and held firm to the boundary. Unfortunately, they had to not only endure Rosie's fury, but the coach was also furious at the thought of losing his key player. The therapist was enlisted to talk to the coach about what was happening and managed to get him on board.

So, as the second week started out like the first, Rosie was enraged. But three days into the second week Rosie shifted. She started eating better and gained one and a half pounds, which they said was enough to play basketball. She went back on the team, they won, and she has stayed on the path of recovery over the following years.

You will see later that McKenzie had something in common with Rosie. When boundaries are set, behavior can change no matter how hopeless it might seem. Rosie's parents did everything right and it worked. They quickly got a treatment team and set boundaries with reward. They started eating with her. This is something we call refeeding or family-based treatment. This was formally called the Maudsley Method, named after a hospital in London where Christopher Dare and colleagues devised the therapy. One study showed an eighty percent success rate. I think having a counselor involved makes it really work.

CHAPTER 4

HOSPITAL

"Without courage, all other virtues lose their value."
- Sir Winston Churchill

What made participating in the ED unit at Research such a great program was, of course, the quality of the staff, including my friend Ellen. But I was numb, I was numb to the fact that I was putting my daughter on the eating disorder unit, a unit that had been alarming to me as their doctor. Now it was so much more alarming, as a mother.

The last time I was in the hospital was when I almost lost McKenzie, at age twelve, a year before we began dealing with her anorexia. It was truly the most terrifying thing that has ever happened to me. It started out with McKenzie experiencing depression. She would draw pictures of how she felt. One of the pictures was so disturbing. It depicted a girl with greasy stringy hair, and a band around her head and chest to represent a tightness she felt. The girl was crying and looked as if she was in despair.

As a psychiatrist, I knew this was a wake-up call. I immediately got her into a child psychiatrist in Portland, Maine where we were living at the time. He started her on Abilify, an antipsychotic, saying it would help regulate her dopamine. I was a little suspicious of his thinking. Didn't she just need an antidepressant like Zoloft or Lexapro? But we tried it. Unfortunately, it made her feel more anxious. She was then put on Lexapro and she started having restless legs, so we stopped after a week. The psychiatrist then started her on Zoloft, but she got more depressed. Nothing seems to be anywhere close to working.

I was now suspecting this depression to be bipolar depression but for some reason he ruled it out. I wanted to change psychiatrists but since we were in the middle of moving back to Kansas City, I decided to wait and get one there. Once situated in Kansas City, I got McKenzie in to see another psychiatrist who agreed with me it could be bipolar since her depression started at such a young age and she had gotten worse on the antidepressant drugs. And most importantly, it runs in the family.

Dr. Lahaye was his name. He started her on Geodon, another antipsychotic. Antipsychotics at that time were popular treatments for bipolar in children. So I guess the psychiatrist in Maine might have been on to something with Abilify. Dr. Lahaye was impressed by how cyclical her depression was, even more support for this being bipolar. Here's where things got scary. McKenzie started to feel a little bit happier on the Geodon, but she was dropping a lot of weight. She kept saying her stomach hurt but thought it might just be her anxiety. I decided to keep her on it while closely monitoring her.

One night, McKenzie was complaining that her stomach was really hurting and she just didn't feel good. So, I had her sleep with me. At about 2 a.m. I suddenly woke up. I looked at McKenzie and I could see that she wasn't breathing. She was limp and unresponsive. I started screaming. I threw her off the bed and called 911 while doing chest compressions. The paramedics were there in four minutes. I didn't think I was getting anywhere but they revived her and put an oxygen mask on her. Off we flew to the hospital. McKenzie now was awake but unaware of what was happening.

When McKenzie finally woke up that night in the hospital, we had flocks of doctors come in to review her case; the only thing they could come up with is that she had the flu. All this perfectly coincided with the swine flu scare in 2009-2010, so they just watched her. She was better but still drowsy. After two days, they had no better answer so sent her home with instructions to watch her closely. Not much help.

When we left, I still was not satisfied with her diagnosis so I started doing my own research. But nothing seemed to fit. The next day at my office one of the secretaries asked about McKenzie. I told her she was still drowsy.

She asked, "Is she on any medications?"

Of course she was, they had kept her on Geodon the entire time. I decided then and there to take her off it. That was the answer. She quickly returned to normal. She was toxic on the Geodon. Incredibly, all those doctors attended her, but none of them thought about it being caused by medication, including me.

This terrifying experience led me to having a baseline of anxiety. I knew life could change in a minute. You could lose someone you love so unexpectedly. We really are so much more vulnerable than we realize. I couldn't shake the fear of losing McKenzie whereas before I never really thought about it.

After the hospitalization, every siren I heard made me fear for my daughter's life. In fact, for months afterwards, I would have a panic attack each time. When this happened, I would usually call the school like a crazy person to make sure my daughter was still alive. I'm sure the school thought I was nuts because I was nuts.

Obviously, I needed to get help for this. So I eventually received EMDR, Eye movement Desensitization Reprocessing Therapy. This is where a person will process their traumatic event while doing specific eye movements. This reprocessing takes the trauma out of the amygdala, which is the fight or flight alarm in the brain, and puts the memory into the frontal lobe where rational thoughts live. Therefore, the memory isn't as emotionally charged.

The EMDR method that was customly made for me was to have me follow a tennis ball on a screen, bouncing back and forth, while I consciously thought about that night when McKenzie stopped breathing. The counselor also played a siren at the same time. In only one appointment I was cured of the siren phobia. EMDR really works so I recommend it for anyone who experiences Post-Traumatic Stress Disorder. The panic with the sound of a siren was gone, but I was still frightened for my daughter's life. When you get so close to losing someone, you realize how vulnerable we are to danger.

Even though McKenzie was off Geodon, I was still petrified she would stop breathing. I had to go upstairs almost every hour while she was sleeping and check on her. This went on for several months, but finally, I started releasing it to God and developed a new life with more appreciation of my daughter. Nevertheless, I would never be completely the same.

Now here it is a little over a year later, and McKenzie and I are back in a hospital. This time, I have just admitted my precious daughter to an eating disorder unit. After about a half hour, I went back upstairs to the unit, thinking that Ellen would probably be done with the examination.

When I got off the elevator they were both there to meet me. Ellen first said she called one of the nurses, Amy, to come in and take care of McKenzie. Amy was my favorite nurse, she was so warm and caring. She made you feel like you were the most important person in the world; the patients loved her.

Ellen asked me to come talk to her in the office.

Once we got settled there, Ellen calmly said, "I think your daughter has anorexia, but I'm going to let Doctor Milgram decide that tomorrow. But I'll tell you what I found on the physical exam."

As she talked, I felt like I was underwater trying to listen. I heard her say that McKenzie had bradycardia, where the heart rate goes down too low, which is usually below 60. A normal rate is 60-100. Bradycardia is a common occurrence in people with anorexia. The heart muscle weakens. McKenzie's rate was 52.

This is important because if the heart slows down too much, there's not enough oxygen to the body and the brain, thus it's possible to have a cardiac arrest. A low heart rate isn't always a problem if you're a trained athlete or healthy young adult but for someone with an eating disorder, it's a problem.

While in the exam, apparently McKenzie had admitted to Ellen that she was having dizziness, weakness, and shortness of breath, all associated with a cardiac condition. Ellen said they were going to have to put her on telemetry, a machine that keeps a running record of the heart rate and rhythm. She said she wanted to keep an eye out for any arrhythmias, which is an abnormal rhythm of the heart which can also be caused by malnourishment. McKenzie also had low blood pressure, 98 over 45. How did this happen? The average blood pressure is 120 over 70. She had so many serious health problems which seemed to happen all of a sudden.

I kept asking myself, "Where were you?" That's all I could think about. My brain was in a fog. Thank God that McKenzie was here at Research because she was in such critical condition. Things had changed so drastically from a week ago when everything appeared to be normal. It just snuck up.

As I sat there with my friend Ellen, I felt like I was listening to information about someone else's daughter. This is called disassociation. It felt traumatic. The trauma I was experiencing was the realization that my daughter might die. It was all happening so fast. I felt like I had just gotten my Mother's Day card.

Now here we are at the hospital. A place which I could possibly leave in a few days without my daughter. Who do I turn to? Could anyone really understand the gravity of all this? For some reason, probably shame, I decided there wasn't anyone to turn to, so I would manage it on my own. Big mistake. This is where, without support, the trauma carved itself into my gut giving me a soccer punch every time I'd think about it from here on out. Not only would it carve itself into my gut but also into my heart so that every time I thought about it I'd almost stop breathing. Not exaggerating.

About this time, Amy, my very favorite nurse, knocked on the door to say hello. She would be the only staff here until Dr. Milgram would arrive the next day. Amy said she was going to help get McKenzie all checked in. I had not seen McKenzie since we got on the unit. I was sure she was just as frightened as I was but, I would soon find out later that she wasn't. I came out of the office to see Amy hand McKenzie her gown and her personal items. I followed McKenzie into her room to say goodbye. She asked me to stay just for a few minutes while she put on her nightgown. She effortlessly took off all her clothes to put on one of those hospital nightgowns.

That's when I saw something I'll never forget. I could see all of my daughter's ribs and her collarbone unnaturally protruding from her chest. She had no waist. She was so thin, it looked like her arms and legs were dangling from her body. I kept asking myself, "Who is going to help her? Someone help her now." I kept referring back to that image I have of her climbing on the bus to kindergarten with her little pixie cut and angelic face. She always wore the same thing, an overall-looking dress with Merrell slip ons. "Help," this was the only prayer I knew for times this bad. It has now been rumored that showing a girl with anorexia a video of herself has much more of an impact on her than a picture.

McKenzie finished putting on her nightgown and kept talking to me rather casually, as if it was just another Monday evening before school. I actually think she was soaking up the attention in some way. The attention that I had deprived her of. She didn't seem to see the seriousness at hand instead talked about how she needed to get her homework.

I don't know what kept her from running. Maybe there was a part of her deep down crying out for help, for attention, to finally be seen. I thought I had been paying attention but not really. I knew I loved her more than life. How were we going to connect? Well, at least for the night, I would fake a smile and hug her good night. I told her how proud of her I was for her staying and not leaving. The drive home was without thought. That numb feeling was still there. My chest was tight and I could hardly breathe.

Once home, I plopped myself into the big red chair and didn't move for at least an hour. I finally decided to get some dinner. I got up, kept everything on including my coat, and fixed some soup. I came back to the chair, and sat, and sat, and finally started thinking about work. I remembered that tomorrow would be Tuesday, and I would have about twenty patients to see. I decided I wasn't in the best shape and called my office manager to rearrange my schedule and see the patients on the upcoming Saturday instead of tomorrow. I felt a little guilty as I remembered what my Aunt Fran would say when I took time off. She was a southern woman who was working for me at the time and was very convincing; she would say that those people needed me, all twenty of them, and I couldn't be selfish. She would say this with the most delicious southern accent so that it was always the gospel. But for the most part she was right, but not this time. I needed to pay attention to my precious, precious daughter.

I looked at the mirror and said, "Not tomorrow, Aunt Fran. Just not tomorrow."

I fell asleep in that big red chair with my coat still on. The next morning, I woke up feeling heavy. I wandered around the house like Frankenstein. I didn't even brush my teeth, and I headed for the hospital. I arrived a little early before the visiting hours at ten, so I got some coffee. At ten, the door opened; McKenzie was waiting for me, excited to tell me about her new psychiatrist. She said his name was Dr. Milgram. She said she loved the way he smelled. Dr. Milgram was a slight man. He was very clean-cut and wore a traditional navy sportcoat with a big red bow tie. Dr. Milgram will always be remembered by his cologne. It was a welcoming smell that predicted his arrival.

He appeared out of nowhere and asked, in a very professional manner, if we could talk.

I hugged McKenzie and said, "Sure." I then followed him into his office.

His office was very organized. He had two diplomas hung up on the wall of his office. One diploma was for his law degree, the other for his psychiatry.

Dr. Milgram sat down behind his desk and I sat in another chair.

After a few minutes, he said that McKenzie was a delight to be with. "Your daughter is a very smart lady, but I am afraid she has anorexia. She meets all the DSM-5 criteria. She has lost a significant amount of weight due to her refusal to eat. She is extremely afraid of getting fat. And she has a disturbance in her perception of her body." He then said something that I couldn't shake. He said, "I am very worried about her."

This was a man who oozed confidence. His words were like glue. I felt dizzy, like I was going to faint. I didn't know if I could handle this moment. This mild-mannered man was very worried and so was I.

Dr. Milgram continued talking and said something not really that surprising. He agreed with Dr. Lahaye that McKenzie might have bipolar II not bipolar I which involves psychosis. I reviewed again in my mind. I knew her depression was unusual because she was so young when it started which is sometimes a sign of bipolar. She also had a very poor response to Zoloft. She became severely depressed with suicidal thinking. Another sign of possible bipolar II. Her depressive episodes were always really severe and would only last three to seven days. In other words she cycled. Just like Dr. Lahaye had said. I kept McKenzie off any medications after the Geodon scare. And for the most part I thought things were ok. I didn't see any significant depression but maybe all her depression channeled through her starvation.

Bipolar II actually runs in the family. My sister has bipolar II. As I said before, it is very genetic. The chance of getting it when one parent has it is fifteen to thirty percent. My sister has been doing well, very successfully, on Lamictal and Seroquel. There probably is bipolar in our ancestry but not ever identified. I had an uncle who was depressed most of his life; sat in his room all day and drew.

I asked Dr. Milgram about hypomania [periods of overactive and high-energy behavior that can have a significant impact on your day-to-day life].

He said yes, and that she had shared a memory with him about a night when she felt she was invincible. She told him she couldn't stop talking about all the things she wanted to do. She said she had a lot of energy that day so she kept running up and down the stairs. She was going to start a babysitting company, make jewelry, and become an astronaut.

I vaguely remember that. She did have a few "hyper" days. But it would only last a few days.

Dr. Milgram then said, "Because I'm suspicious of it, I would like to put her on a mood stabilizer?" He wanted to know if I would mind him doing this.

I said, "No, I don't mind."

It all made sense because there usually is another comorbid mental illness associated with anorexia. Other comorbidities include depression, obsessive compulsive disorder and substance dependency. Maybe treating this would really help.

Dr. Milgram said, "I'd like to try Lamictal."

I liked that idea. It was my favorite mood stabilizer to use with my patients since it has such few side effects.

Apparently, according to Dr. Milgram McKenzie, had completely stopped eating food three weeks ago. She was throwing all the food away when I wasn't looking. She had also been exercising every day; riding the stationary bike while I was at work for up to two hours sometimes. Two hours seemed unbelievable; then I thought back to the patient doing crunches under her hospital bed. The drive to lose weight was an obsession with no end.

Dr. Milgram then said that McKenzie did not feel she would ever be as successful as everyone else in the family. That triggered a memory. About three weeks ago, I was sitting in the car in our driveway with McKenzie. I had just picked her up from tennis practice. We had a very serious discussion about sports. I hope I can repeat it word by word here in this book; it was a turning point for McKenzie.

Me: "How was practice?"

McKenzie: "Oh, just okay."

Me: "You don't sound very excited about it."

McKenzie: "I can't get my forehand to work."

Me: "Honey, it just takes more practice."

McKenzie: "Mom, I am not really good at anything. I need to be good at something. Everyone in the Willson family is good at a sport. Uncle Mark played college football, Aunt Alise played college softball. Grandpa played college football and basketball, and you, of course, played college tennis. Also, all my cousins are really good at sports. I can't find anything I'm really good at. Mom, I need something!" She then started crying.

I remember feeling her pain and hearing it in her voice. I knew that sports were like a religion in our family. I didn't realize how much pressure that would put on her.

She then broke down and kept saying, "I need to find something that's mine. I am not good at anything."

Now looking back, I see the gravity of the situation. A light bulb went off. That was why and when all this had started. She was finally good at something. She was good at being thin.

CHAPTER 5

LOST

"When we lose God, it is not God who is lost."
- Unknown

After my discussion with Dr. Milgram, who I decided I already loved, I went to find McKenzie. She was in the dining room with her counselor, Carrie. McKenzie was required to eat all her meals with the nurse or a counselor. Every meal included something from all four food groups, plus an Ensure. They had to eat the entire meal as well as the Ensure. Carrie actually had a history of an eating disorder herself, but looked great now. I sat down next to my daughter, who was saying to Carrie that she couldn't eat anymore. So eating a full meal wasn't just a mere suggestion; it was flat-out forbidden not to eat everything on your plate, which was a starch, a meat, a vegetable, and a fruit, topped off with dessert, and don't forget that Ensure.

Carrie was firm; she said, "McKenzie, you need to eat everything."

McKenzie picked and picked at her food until she was finished with everything except the desert and the Ensure, which she refused to drink. She said, "You're making me fat."

Carrie finally acquiesced and took the tray away.

I looked at McKenzie and again said, "Are you kidding me? You really think you're fat?"

She replied, "Of course, Mom. Look at me," while pointing to her flat stomach.

We walked back to her room and by then only had a few minutes to talk. We spent most of the time sorting out the clothes I had brought. I didn't want to belabor the point of her not finishing her meal. I was going to let the staff do that. But I couldn't help but ask her how she could think she was fat when she weighed ninety-five pounds! She turned away from me and kept putting away her clothes. Frustrated that she still has this illusion about her body, I decided not to say anything else.

How could someone so logical and smart believe this lie? McKenzie scored very high on all the standardized testing. She made straight As and was always one of the teacher's favorites because she was so well-behaved. But right now it seemed that she could be considered delusional. I had seen this pattern of irrational thinking with my patients and often wondered if they wouldn't benefit from an antipsychotic. They too were usually perfectionists. Straight A students. Responsible young ladies. Same as McKenzie. I don't get it.

I decided I was not going to bring up her weight again until someone told me how to talk to her about it so I just turned and left her room. Apparently, they had had two more admissions that morning to the ED unit. Just as I stepped into the hallway, two young girls about McKenzie's age were heading down the hall to the group room.

I turned back into McKenzie's room and she quickly said, "Mom, I don't want to go."

As evenly as possible I said, "Of course you don't. But this is probably the most important thing you do, next to eating, so you need to go." And then I added, "I am not leaving until you go."

She sulked for a moment, but reluctantly went down the hall waving her hand goodbye.

I stayed in McKenzie's room for a little while and laid on the bed, trying to take a deep breath, wondering what to do with myself. I finally got up and headed for the elevator. I decided I was going to go see my mom. I got to the ground floor and headed for my car, again still feeling that dull numbness. What was I going to say to my mom? I decided that it was time to tell her everything. I really needed someone to confide in. Once in the car I quickly called to see if I could come over and she said, "Sure," so I headed that way.

Once I got to the house, I blurted out the bald fact right away, "Mom, McKenzie has anorexia."

And Mom said very, very seriously, "What exactly is that?"

I said, "It's an eating disorder where you starve yourself. Can't you tell how thin she is?"

Mom said, "But thin is normal at her age. She just wants to look good."

I said, "Mom, that's not all there is. She feels like she's fat when she's thin, and she's not eating because she feels like she's fat. It's very dangerous. She has heart problems because of it."

My mom again said, "Honey, all these girls are thin."

I couldn't believe it. My mom was not going to take this seriously. I felt my heart sink. How could she not see it herself? At least believe me, right? This was going to be the only person I really turned for that deep true support and it was failing. Would it fail everywhere? I really was in this alone. Oh, and also very angry. I tried several times and different ways of explaining this serious illness to my mom but no bite. I couldn't get through to my mom how very serious this was but, it wasn't that surprising. Mom would protect herself from painful things by denying it. In some ways it worked at times so she could keep going but this time I needed her heart. It wasn't that she didn't believe me. She actually couldn't believe me; it was too scary. She was the one I confided in. I could tell she wasn't going to change her mind so I decided to leave.

When I got home, I spent the rest of the night researching anorexia. I have researched it before but now I have a whole different type of motivation. Such as what might be up ahead. The most striking thing to me is how the brain changes when someone goes into starvation mode; the brain actually tells the person that they need to stop eating, even though their body is starved. They stop getting those hunger calls. It is an interesting paradox and hard to break once a person gets to such a low weight. We are working against the powerful brain. The question now isn't whether the brain does this, it is why.

There is evidence that in the concentration camps the starving prisoners would just lose their interest in food. Likely the same neural pathway as that for anorexia. They have done MRIs on young girls with anorexia and seen a change in their frontal lobe which is where you do all your critical thinking. The frontal lobe returned to normal once they gained weight. I will talk about this more when we go into the clinical part of anorexia.

I just sat there in my big red chair for over an hour looking up everything I could about anorexia. The things that kept standing out were that back in

2013 it seemed to be thought of by some as a family disease particularly the mom. Now anorexia is thought of by most psychiatrists as being a biological disease. Brain scans of the frontal lobes of individuals with anorexia are different from the average individual but as I said before, turn around once nourished.

When alone I didn't like to listen to music or the TV. I was so anxious that everything annoyed me. I thought about calling some of my friends just to talk but didn't know what to really say. How to start out a conversation such as "How are you?" and I would answer "I think I am going to die from the great pain I am feeling." Everything felt too serious. So deep that I was drowning in it. I still hadn't brought up the situation with McKenzie to anyone but Mom. It was too painful and somehow, embarrassing.

I didn't understand how people could keep on going while this horrific thing was happening to my sweet daughter. I feel I am being suffocated by fear and sadness. How do I keep going? I have to be strong for McKenzie. I need to keep working. I sometimes just want a big tranquilizer to help me forget about this pain.

Exhausted, I finally just ate my familiar two peanut butter and jelly sandwiches with tomato soup and felt overwhelmed knowing I would have to see patients in the morning. It was all I could do to just crawl into bed, still wearing the same clothes from two days ago. Still no shower. Just couldn't do it. My daughter might die. That thought paralyzed me. I just couldn't move my body to do anything but drive and somehow to see patients.

Somehow, I was able to get it together the next morning. I took a shower, put on something casual, and headed to the office. I guess, like every other professional, I knew how to be a professional when it was required. I could backseat my emotions for at least eight hours and somehow, it didn't interfere with my focus on the patients. They came first. They were willing to talk to someone about how they felt and I was lucky enough to be that someone. I was always honored.

The practice was still growing. I had lots of support in my office. I had a new nurse practitioner, Pam Pierce, who made my day so much easier. She knew what we were going through and upped her game. My office manager was also aware and very supportive. I still knew how to diagnose, and get a treatment plan together. Thank God.

So I got through the day without any problems and headed for Research again. This time when I got to the unit, McKenzie was waiting for me with Dr. Milgram and the counselor. Oh my God, what was wrong? I wanted to run. I felt panicked. I started to sweat. Suddenly, I didn't want to be a parent.

Dr. Milgram directed us into the dining room.

After we sat down, he said, "McKenzie has lost another pound. She has refused to finish most of her meals and doesn't drink the Ensure. We are really worried about her so I think we need to put a feeding tube in to give her a head start."

I knew that some of my partners had to do this with their patients but not me. I blankly stared back without a reply, feeling the panic turn to rage.

I finally said, "Of course."

I had never been so mad at my daughter as I was right then and there. She was playing Russian roulette with her life and I had to sit back and just watch.

All I could do was mutter, "Oh my god, of course."

Right then I was very grateful for the doctor's experience and expertise, but realized I was scared to death of seeing a tube stuck down my daughter's throat. Plus, maybe I was still in shock because of the reason they had to do it: McKenzie was severely malnourished. I couldn't believe it. My daughter who I had a few days prior thought was doing so great. Making her As. This had really blindsided me. I was now thinking I was going to leave the hospital without her forever. After working through my internal emotional whirlwind, I felt the grief just settle in my body.

Right now you might be asking yourself when can I learn more about this disease? One in every four people knows someone who has had an eating disorder. Especially if you have a child between the ages of twelve to eighteen. And since Covid, the statistics show even younger children, eight to eleven, have it.

In 2022, there were twice as many hospitalizations for anorexia. And up to 10,000 deaths that year doubled from the year before. Social media, such as Instagram or Facebook, is the greatest contributor as it slaps these young girls in the face everyday. The girls with the perfect bodies are the girls out there having fun. Not the dumpy ones. Really, no girl at the age of twelve is excited to see her body start curving with the promise of adolescence.

At least a third of all deaths related to anorexia are from cardiac causes. Like I said before, starvation can weaken the walls of the heart, leading to complications. Suicide represents the second leading cause of death. People with anorexia are eighteen times more likely than their peers to commit suicide. And thirdly, electrolyte imbalance can cause seizures and death.

When you are a parent with a teenager, you need to be vigilantly watching for challenges, especially eating problems with girls. What is the difference between a girl who just wants to lose weight, like eighty-five percent of the girls want to, and a girl who has possible anorexia? Eating disorder specialist and clinical psychologist, Michael Strober, said there are three stages. They are: "innocent dieting," where the teen might start watching their calorie intake but do nothing much more. The second stage is called "exhilarated dieting," where the teen actually starts getting a boost when lowering food intake. And third is when the teen becomes "obsessed and preoccupied with dieting." This is when dieting turns into starvation.

So once aware, you need to get your team. I started out with a nutritionist, which is fine if you feel your child isn't in serious trouble. But if your child is starving themself and already down to a low weight, I recommend getting a doctor as well. The nutritionist might just be a place to start as the denial is so deep that a nutritionist might be the only one your child will see. Like McKenzie, she was willing to go see Katie but of course not to the hospital.

In picking out a doctor, try to get someone who specializes in eating disorders, usually a psychiatrist. *Psychology Today* is a good place to start as it sorts out the clinicians by their specialties. What you certainly need is someone who will weigh your child and know what to do with that information. Someone who can calculate a BMI. Remember, it has to be 18.5 or higher.

If you are looking for possible anorexia the BMI might be in a normal range, but there could be other signs. (See Chapter 2 for a complete list.) The main signs include significant weight loss, refusal to eat, and almost always eating alone. Someone with anorexia or possible anorexia finds starving themself as a sense of competence. Once I knew McKenzie's BMI was so low it was obvious that she had to be hospitalized. This is the right thing to do, however, I also had a friend who could help make that happen. Here's some things you can do.

As I said before, there are eating disorder screening apps that immediately get you into contact with the National Eating Disorders Association (NEDA) if you test positive for anorexia. Or you can contact NEDA yourself. They are located in New York City. The phone number is (212) 575-6200. They will help you with getting resources and a physician. If you are in immediate need of help, you can call the crisis line at 988.

Please note that if your child is under eighteen and is in a life-threatening condition, a physician who specializes in eating disorders will be able to hospitalize the patient by court order to get them fed. Remember, at this point the child is not thinking rationally and so can be found incompetent to make their own decisions. Forcing your child to eat is the right thing but it won't feel like it at the time. If your child still has a normal BMI and is willing to eat, start with eating together as many meals as possible. If the child is starting to starve themself, not only should you start to eat meals with them but you must get a counselor. When looking for a counselor, I recommend getting one who does cognitive-behavioral therapy (CBT); it's been identified as the best therapy for anorexia. It takes dysfunctional thoughts and behavioral cycles and replaces it with healthy, more rational thinking and behavior. For example, if someone says, "I feel fat, so I'm going to stop eating," you ask "What's the evidence or the support for being fat?" You point out that there is no evidence. Trying to change these irrational thoughts of being fat to being skinny evidenced by weight and clothing size. This shift in thought can change feelings which can change behavior. CBT done with the right counselor can be very effective.

CHAPTER 6

COMPLICATIONS

"Knowing others is wisdom. Knowing yourself is enlightenment."

- Lao-tzu

Back at Research Hospital, we were not out of the woods. After discussing the need to use a feeding (nasogastric) tube, Dr. Milgram asked if I would stay and help support McKenzie when they put the tube in. Naturally, I said yes and took my coat off with plans to stay for a while. I had no idea what it was going to be like. I knew from seeing other patients with tubes that they were very uncomfortable.

I went into McKenzie's room where I found her pacing saying, "Mom, I will not let them do this to me."

I firmly said, "McKenzie, we are going to save your life whether you like it or not. I'm telling you we are definitely going to do this, and I will hold your hand all the way through it."

Finally, with the encouragement of Dr. Milgram, McKenzie agreed to the feeding tube. I thought they would have to call in the hospital IV team but apparently they had done this before so Dr. Milgram and Amy planned to do it right after lunch. I had to call the office and cancel my patients so I could be beside McKenzie when they put in her feeding tube. So around 1 p.m., the team gathered around McKenzie's bed with a long, clear, coiled tube about the width of four big straws.

The goal was to put it in McKenzie's nose, down the back of her throat, and into her stomach. At first, she kept pulling it out because it was too uncomfortable but finally, they brought in her counselor, Carrie, who had clicked right away with McKenzie. She and I softly coaxed McKenzie through the process while she gagged the entire way until they thought they had it to the point where they wanted to check the location.

The doctor used a stethoscope to listen to make sure it was in the stomach and not in the lungs. He pushed a little air through the tube and then listened with the stethoscope again to make sure it was in the right place. We were all relieved that it was correctly placed, so they taped it to her nose to keep it in place. McKenzie would have that tube taped to her nose for a whole week. But thank God for the quick decisions and skilled work done by her team. Again, they kept saving my daughter's life.

I spent the rest of the afternoon in McKenzie's room while she attended two group sessions. By this point there were three more patients, so there were a total of four in the group with one counselor. McKenzie told me that two of the girls were about her age, the other was around thirty-five. The thirty-five-year-old had been hospitalized six times before this one. McKenzie said one of the girls had terrible OCD. Whenever she saw a flat surface she had to touch it three times and no medications were helping. The other two both had depression and were on new medications. McKenzie said they had a lot in common. None of them wanted to eat. Only McKenzie had a feeding tube. This left her choking a lot when she talked. After a few weeks, I think the groups were really helping because McKenzie was starting to want to eat. More likely it was also the fact that she was starting to get nourished so her brain was coming around. She actually started looking forward to the meals. McKenzie was getting better. After three weeks, she had gained five pounds and now weighed 100. Her heart rate started going up as well, back to 75. Thank God she never had any arrhythmias. She did remain constipated. The nurses were constantly giving her enemas, but Dr. Milgram said this was common. McKenzie was now participating better. Getting the feeding tube out likely helped that.

There are biopsychosocial aspects involved in anorexia. Which means there is a biological part, a psychological part, and a social part. In looking at anorexia, the biological part is the change in the brain chemistry. The psychological part is the need to control their emotions. And the social part is their need to be liked and noticed for being skinny.

I would see patients from 8 a.m. to 3 p.m. with a long lunch break so I could participate in some of the lectures for families that were offered. One was particularly good. It was done by a woman who had been in recovery for twenty years. She said starving yourself was a way of gaining control while in emotional turmoil. She compared it to being in a fast flowing river and finding a branch from a tree to hang on to. It really started to ring true with everything I had learned about anorexia. This made sense to why McKenzie sought it as help for her emotional despair around her lack of a strong identity.

I had just started a clinic called The Purple Door from scratch with the help of my southern Aunt Fran who was a good accountant but knew nothing about medicine or psychiatry. She said it would be impossible for me to find a biller I could trust. So she got out her legal pad and started answering my phone. She set up appointments and billed the insurance. Within three years, I had three nurse practitioners, three counselors, and one office manager. By the time I closed the practice after seven years, I had 800 patients. My Aunt Fran worked for four of those years and never asked for a penny. She died of congestive heart failure a few years ago. Boy, did I love that woman. She said she helped me out because I was a good doctor and was helping a lot of people.

When McKenzie got sick with her eating disorder, my practice was on a roll. People were coming from as far away as Oklahoma. I enjoyed each and every patient I had. They all had a story. I had such joy and enthusiasm but it all started to slowly change when McKenzie got sick. When I was home alone while McKenzie was in the hospital, I still spent a lot of time in the big red chair. I didn't even watch TV. That was too stimulating. I just rested. Tried to calm my nerves. Looking back, I don't even know if I actually changed my clothes every day.

One day I decided to start swimming in the mornings. I needed to do something with my anxiety. So I drove to the neighborhood YMCA and swam twenty to fifty laps every morning. This seemed to relax me. It helped for a while but unfortunately when the anxiety got worse, I was too frozen with fear to do anything besides my practice and being at the hospital. For me, every day that McKenzie was still alive was a miracle. Her heart was struggling to beat. Her stomach was trying to function, and her electrolytes were trying to stabilize. It felt surreal like we were hanging on by our fingernails every single day.

I also learned a very important lesson about myself. I couldn't be vulnerable. I certainly didn't have a counselor. Unfortunately, this made the trauma so much more debilitating for me. I could have talked to my close friends more and asked for their support. I could have gone to a counselor who specializes in eating disorders or found a supportive group, even if online. I was so alone and scared. This is why I want to help other parents do the right things as soon as possible. I want to emphasize that people should not be ashamed of the illness; it is more common than what is talked about.

CHAPTER 7

PSYCHOLOGICAL

"As soon as you trust yourself, you will know how to live."

The psychological part, in my opinion, is the most important part of the bio-psychosocial model of anorexia. So, in McKenzie's case, the statement she made on the driveway after tennis practice was so important. It is the vital factor. Where she said she had to be good at something because everyone in the family has something they are good at. She became good at being skinny.

Let's look at the developmental stage she would be in according to Erik Erikson's psychosocial model of stages. Erik Erikson was a psychoanalyst and professor at Harvard who became the most popular and influential psychologist with his stages of development. His model replaced Sigmund Freud's psychosexual development. Children who are preteen to teen ages are in stage four of development which has the conflict of industry versus inferiority. Whether one develops a sense of competency or not. So important. So when you are looking at these preteens to teenage children assess them to see if they are mastering anything. Here are all the stages.

Erikson's Developmental stages

    Stage 1: Trust versus Mistrust Stage

    Stage 2: Autonomy versus Shame

    Stage 3: Initiative versus Guilt Stage

    Stage 4: Industry versus Inferiority

    Stage 5: Identity versus Role Confusion

Stage 6: Intimacy versus Isolation

Stage 7: Generativity versus Stagnation

Stage 8: Integrity versus Despair

We are going to give attention to stage four and five. First stage four, Industry versus Inferiority. If successful here, development leads to the virtue of competence. Feeling like you are good at something. You can master something like reading or writing. It can be sports, art, photography, bowling, debate, or just being good at relationships.

With this sense of competence comes identity stage 5. If they don't find an area of competency, they have role confusion. They don't think they can manage things. Success breeds success. They need to see themself master something to believe they can manage something else. With McKenzie, grades didn't help her identity enough for some reason. Maybe because middle school doesn't seem to be as impressive with grades compared to high school. So maybe at a later age, it would satisfy that sense of competency.

How do we help these young girls find their competency and subsequent identity? We first have to identify their qualities and talents. Acknowledge their accomplishments when they happen. One school that identified twelve kids with depression put them into a photography class and then hung their photos all over the school. Eight out of twelve of the children's depression lifted.

These talents can be what I listed above. It can even be having good leadership and relationship skills.

One thing I thought might be good is to send cards to all the girls 12-18 that you know and write out what you notice they are so good at. For example, "McKenzie, you are so good at making people happy." Or "McKenzie you are smart at math." Reiterate all the things you notice they are good at. And if you can't currently find something, you need to go find it. Especially with someone who has possible anorexia. They need to find their identity apart from being thin and as fast as you can.

CHAPTER 8

DISCHARGE

"There is no medicine like hope, no incentive so great, and no tonic so powerful as expectation of something tomorrow."

- Unknown

McKenzie was discharged from Research Medical Center one month after admission. She got her feeding tube out after a week and then started eating well with her nurse or counselor watching her at first then she was able to eat on her own the last two weeks. She started eating everything on her plate plus an Ensure. During this long month, I feel like we both gained a generous amount of information about her anorexia. Dr. Milgram said he thought McKenzie's starvation was due to three things.

One, she was suffering from bipolar depression which improved some with the Lamictal, but it was still at a low dose. Lamictal is a medication you have to titrate up slowly or you can get a Stevens Johnson rash which can be fatal. You start at 25mg and double every two and a half weeks. McKenzie had been on 50mg for the last week, but needed to get up to 200mg to be therapeutic. At 100mg, it can be doubled after one week so she still has two weeks to go.

The second of the three things he thought contributed to her starvation was her low self-esteem, which he thinks started when we moved from Maine to Kansas where she lost some friends at a crucial age. The reason we moved to Kansas was because my mom, who lived in Kansas, was suffering from Parkinson's and I wanted to be nearby. Also, I wanted McKenzie to go to Shawnee Mission East. It has an excellent reputation as a public school and it is where I graduated from.

The third thing that Dr. Milgram mentioned was her loneliness at home. She was alone from 3 to 7 p.m., when I got home. Dinnertime was always delayed till later which was not so good. We didn't have a set schedule to share meals. I had a plan to rectify all these things.

As I am also trained as a forensic psychiatrist; I know how to assess risk of violence so I just applied it to risk for relapse. You pick the risk factors you can change and address them. You can not change risk factors that are called static risk factors. For example, you can't change genetics or history if that is a risk factor. Like previous violence is a risk factor for future violence but you can't change it. An example of what you can change is the use of substances which doubles the risk for violence.

Here are the things that put McKenzie at a risk for relapse. Her risk factors again were bipolar, loneliness, and a lack of identity. We were treating bipolar. I needed to be home earlier for dinner to help prevent her loneliness, but the third thing was going to be the hardest, identity. Remember, she told us that she feels she is not good at anything so instead of having competency (industry) she has inferiority. And if we also look at stage five of Erikson's model, this lack of competency flows into her not having an identity: identity as a tennis player, etc. My challenge was how to help McKenzie get a beautiful, normalized identity for herself instead of being identified as "the skinny girl". She still claimed that she loved the skinny identity and was still fighting it when we left the hospital. All these risk factors were about to change.

My precious McKenzie left Research at age thirteen, still beautiful, and weighing 105 pounds. She spent a little more than one month in the hospital. The treatment plan was to continue to gain one to two pounds a week up to an ideal weight of 115 pounds with a BMI of 18.6. We were to follow up with a new counselor named Ashley and go back to meeting with Katie the nutritionist. I was excited to have a team when we left, but I was still running around scared to death.

McKenzie is still very vulnerable to a relapse so let's look at major risk factors and see if we are managing them well. Her first one is bipolar which we are treating with Lamictal. The second risk factor is her self-esteem, which we will be looking at things McKenzie can achieve in. The third one is loneliness. I plan to be home every night while we eat together.

CHAPTER 9

DECISIONS

"You must have long-range goals to keep you from being frustrated by short-term failures."

- Charles C. Noble

McKenzie and I left the hospital ready to start a whole new life together. Of course, we were still not completely on the same page. Once home, McKenzie said she would try to follow the treatment plan which was to continue to gain weight but was very resistant to gaining ten more pounds. This is where she stayed stuck. I believe if I would have caught it earlier, we would be where Rosie and her family ended up. A full recovery after boundaries were initially set. But I am also aware that, unlike Rosie, McKenzie did not have the identity of being a basketball star. I had really needed to intervene sooner with a game plan when she told me she was not good at anything.

I believe if I would have noticed it sooner, we might have been able to turn it around before the new anorexia neural pathways were laid down. Research shows that something practiced for twenty-one days can lay down a specific memory for that activity. This was exactly the amount of time McKenzie had been working on her weight loss.

The other obvious thing was not eating meals together. There are several studies that report eating together as a family, what they call "refeeding", has a lot of success. Off we went. We started our life together at the kitchen table where our relationship would experience many ups and downs. I would say McKenzie was halfway there. But you will find out soon why halfway isn't good enough.

I was told by Mckenzie's counselor and Dr. Milgram to set a tough boundary. For example, this would always include a full dinner with a snack. McKenzie chose energy bars instead of Ensure as her snack. Now you know it is obvious I won't be able to eat with her at lunch, but we did eat breakfast and dinner together. I noticed when we had our dinners together that McKenzie really picked at her food. Something I really wasn't expecting. I didn't see how she was going to get to 115 pounds, but soon the answer came.

McKenzie was originally hospitalized two days before school was to be let out. So they let her go ahead and graduate from Indian Hills. She was headed to Shawnee Mission East. The reason I moved back from Maine was to get McKenzie into what I think is one of the best public schools in the country. After she was home from the ED unit, we had one month to prepare for this grand opening.

Two weeks after discharge, McKenzie met with Ashley and Katie alone. I followed up with a phone call to see if they thought she had made any progress. They both said not really. They weren't allowed to discuss any details since they had therapeutic confidentiality. So how were we going to move forward any more?

Shawnee Mission East is known for its strong academics but also a lot for it's sports. So when school started, I wanted McKenzie to give sports one more try, so I told her she had to pick a fall sport. I told her about the ones that were "no cut" and she liked that idea. She decided on cross country. I was surprised at that but decided to just wait to see what would happen.

Three days into school, she came running into my clinic screaming. I happened to be available so I quickly came out of my office to see what was going on. McKenzie was jumping up and down with my office staff.

She said, "Mom, I placed in the top twenty girls."

At first, I was kind of puzzled. I didn't have any idea what she was talking about.

She quickly explained through her rapid breathing. "Mom, cross country."

She said she had gone out for cross country the day before and was told to bring running clothes the next day. Well, guess what? They had all the girls, freshman through seniors, run at one time to see who were the fastest. McKenzie finished in the top twenty of all these girls who have been running cross country for the last four years. I will say it again because I have never been prouder. McKenzie finished in the top twenty out of the entire school of girls.

This was a kid who finished last place in the mile in fourth grade. God now gave her this gift. The gift to run. She was becoming noticed and now knows she has potential for something big. I couldn't be happier. I was done for the day so I gave her a ride home. I had never seen her in such a good mood. This is a girl that tried hard at basketball, swimming, lacrosse, and tennis and just didn't seem to find a fit. I knew that with hard work she had found her sport, but didn't know if she was willing to work for it. Talent only gives you a head start. It is the one who practices who actually becomes the best. I knew this from tennis.

I was the worst in my tennis class at camp when I was thirteen years old. I could do all the other sports without any trouble. I was the pitcher for our softball team, and I was one of the fattest in my class. I also played basketball like a boy. But I was terrible at tennis. So this made me try even harder. I went up to our local park where there were tennis courts that included a backboard. I would practice on it for hours. Then I would play with anyone who would play with me. I think some of the men I played with even lived in their cars in the park. I didn't care. With time I got a lot better. I ended up winning state doubles and then going on to play college tennis at the University of Kansas on scholarship. That is when the real work began. Practice for two hours was just the beginning. We did sprints and jumped rope for as long as our legs could handle. Then I would play anytime I could outside of practice. It was hard work but I loved it. I am not sure how my past with sports affected McKenzie's need for recognition but I imagine it did influence her.

McKenzie and I went home with her chatting the whole way. When I started preparing dinner, my chattering brain kicked in. I started thinking about how much weight someone could lose running. McKenzie had only gained a pound since she left the program. According to Katie, who we saw right a week after discharge, she now weighed 106 pounds. I only weighed her once a week at the advice of the team.

Maybe it wasn't such a great idea to participate in a sport where she would lose more weight. How was I going to tell her no? I was quiet through dinner thinking of how to tell her. Later that evening while in my big red chair, it hit me that running cross country could actually be an incentive to gain weight or not be able to run. Now this would be a challenge, but was what we needed because McKenzie was still lost. She needed to feel important. To have identity. I was so excited I found an idea that would possibly work. I knew that she might slip back without a reason for gaining weight. Oddly enough, cross country would help. I had to wrestle with this decision.

So I asked McKenzie what she liked about running. She cheerfully said that she got to be with her friends. It helped her mood to run, especially outside. And most of all she was proud. These were all good reasons. So after dinner I decided to let her run. I ran upstairs to tell her how happy I was, but that she would have to maintain a weight of 110-115. She looked at me for a minute then smiled. We both started jumping up and down. It was a very happy moment in the midst of all the pain.

CHAPTER 10

CROSS COUNTRY

"Great Works are performed not by strength, but by perseverance."
- Unknown

There is nothing more exciting than seeing your child run. She ran through the country with such endurance and speed, I would try to see her as many times as I could. Peeking through the trees with all the other parents. My heart was racing. I was always so nervous. Here is a running story written by McKenzie herself.

I was nervous to start my freshman year of high school (ninth grade) because the last time any of my classmates had seen me was pre-hospitalization for my ED. I was hospitalized during the last month of my eighth-grade year. I worried that my extremely low weight and month-long absence from school would be the elephant in the room when I would interact with my peers. It was mortifying to think. However, I figured that another reason kids think I might have disappeared from school was I had a "legitimate" illness that secondarily caused me to become sickly and thin. I decided not to dwell on what others might have conjectured about my absence because I could not let myself go down that rabbit hole or else I would never be able to go back to school.

The reason I decided to try out for cross country was because of my best friend at the time. She was an excellent swimmer and cross country was a great way to cross-train during the off-season. Since I wanted to play basketball in the winter, I thought cross country would be a great way for me to cross-train during the off-season as well. And it was a no cut sport.

The same day I learned about cross country was also the first official day of practice. I hadn't even brought a pair of running shoes with me to school that day, so I technically had to skip the first day of practice. I don't remember what my first pair of running shoes were because I did not put much thought into which brand or style would be the best. For the first few practices, we ran three miles at most. I don't recall ever running farther than one mile prior to cross country and the one mile I had run was required for PE class in middle school.

Our team's formal timed trial would take place in a few weeks on an early Saturday morning at a local park. In the meantime, to get a general idea of the team standings, the coaches held an informal timed trial after practice one day. I can still remember the prescribed course. It was a winding, relatively scenic route through the neighborhoods adjacent to our high school. Since I had been running with my best friend during practices, I started the race alongside her.

Everyone (boys and girls) started the trial together. So many kids shot off at the start of the race. I thought how could that be sustainable?

Don't we have to run two whole miles? My friend and I started off at a fast enough pace that we could not keep a conversation but not so fast that we were full-on sprinting. About a third of a mile into the trial, most of the kids who had started the race off sprinting had run out of steam and slowed to an easy jog. Simultaneously, I felt a surge of energy and thought I could go at a little faster pace. I could not believe what was transpiring.

How did I have so much energy? I looked at the runners ahead of me. I wondered if I could catch up with them. Once I reach the runner(s) in front of me, I aim to catch up with the next. I felt like I was flying. I felt powerful.I don't remember exactly where I placed in the first timed trial, but I know I qualified (unofficially) for JV which meant I finished in the top twenty girls. After the trial, I beamed with happiness and awe. I remember specifically going to my mom's work right after cross-country practice.

Even though I knew she would be busy seeing a patient, I could not contain my excitement. I waited in her office manager's office while she finished the appointment with her patient. When her door opened, I gave her a wave from across the hall to signal I was there. After she said goodbye to her patient she came to see why I was at the office and I told her I unofficially qualified for the JV cross country team. My mom echoed my surprise and we celebrated. By the end of my sophomore year, I earned a spot on the varsity squad.

During the summer before my junior year, I went to my team's training practices every morning. Looking back, I don't know how I maintained the will and dedication to go to practice every day at 7 a.m. for eight weeks. And rarely did any of the other girl's varsity runners attend the summer practices, so I often ran alone or I ran with the boy's varsity team (who had many more regular attendees than the girl's varsity). Even though I do not remember feeling sad that summer, the whole experience was objectively a very lonely one and I think had I been more in touch with my emotions, I would not have been able to practice the way I did.

The official cross-country season started in August. The hard work I put in over the summer showed in my race times. I would finish a whole two minutes before the next girl on the team. I set the school record. I was featured on the front page of the school newspaper. I was on top of the world. My cross-country season junior year is still one of the best times of my life. I wonder how my season might have been different had I been at a healthier weight. I was clearly not quite at a healthy, athletic weight. Unfortunately, my coach was indifferent about my nutrition and if I was fueling myself enough. There is a common misconception that being underweight is advantageous for my competitive running and I think my coach probably believed it as well. Had I been better fueled, I wonder if I could have run even faster. Though I did finish twenty-second at state, one of my biggest regrets is not fueling better during the season and believing that thinner equals faster. I bet I could have had the endurance and kick to finish in the top twenty at state.

Malnutrition finally came back to bite me in the butt during my senior year. I was still running just as fast as my junior year but I got plagued with a stress fracture mid-season and failed to qualify for state. I ran the race at regionals even though my team, coaches, and I all knew I had a stress fracture. I knew I would not run as fast but I could boost the chances of my team possibly qualifying for state even if I finished 5th on our team. Point-scoring for cross country is very complicated and I still don't even know how it works.)

The pain was excruciating and I did not finish first on the team like usual but rather seventh. We did not qualify for state as a team, but my coaches were proud of me for gritting through the pain and being a true team player. There is a post-race photo of me with my teammates jumping in the air and by that point, the pain in my leg from the stress fracture was so intense that I was the only one not mid-jump in the picture because I could not bear the thought of a hop on my injured leg.

I love that picture because even though my teammates were disappointed to not qualify for state, they were clearly so happy and proud to finish a great season. Looking back on the picture helped to give me closure for a season that was disappointing performance-wise but was incredibly fulfilling team-mate-wise. I became so close with the other girls on the team and made so many great memories with my teammates, unlike my lonely junior year or any other year, honestly. All in all, the last two seasons of my cross-country career were great for two different reasons and I am thankful for both.

CHAPTER 11

THE FINISH LINE

"If you don't stand for something, you'll fall for anything"
 - Michael Evans

I loved every minute of cross country. It brought McKenzie and I a lot closer. McKenzie ended up making the varsity with only one other freshman. Pretty amazing. After about three weeks of practice they started competing. So there was a meet every Saturday rain or shine including temperatures above 100. So at the first meet, I was so nervous and yet proud. All the girls lined up on one line then the gun went off and off they went. It was a 4k which was two and a half miles. They ran it like it was a sprint. Boy they took off without holding back. Not even one.

McKenzie was always nervous the night before and would usually ask me if she had to run. I always said absolutely not. That seemed to settle her down enough where she could go to sleep, get up the next morning and actually not only run but run well.

McKenzie was the steady one who could run forever. She was always working on her kick. Boy, would I yell loud when she was rounding that last turn. "Kick McKenzie kick!"

Coach Trish was always satisfied with her times the first year in running. Expectations changed a little as she moved on up to be sophomore, junior than senior.

A few days after McKenzie made the team she had an appointment with Katie, her nutritionist. I wasn't in the appointment but apparently when

McKenzie told Katie she was going to be running cross country it did not sit well. Which I can understand at face value why it would seem wrong.

McKenzie wasn't having any of those dark days like she had in the past. There was no hypomania either. Lamictal must be working. And I think it is fair to say she has bipolar. I think now was a good time for her to dive into therapy. She started with a woman named Ashley.

McKenzie was so proud to run for her school. She loved to put on her uniform. What she didn't like so much was the pressure from me to keep eating. I at least wanted her to reach 110 pounds. She was now 108 so to give her credit she had made progress. This wasn't easy running three to five miles a day. McKenzie had the same thing every night. A piece of chicken, some broccoli and a sweet potato followed by her protein bar.

This really wasn't enough so I tried to get her to eat a dessert but she wouldn't. She only would eat three things: chicken, broccoli, and sweet potatoes. Followed by a protein bar. The problem with all of this is the portions were always very small. We were not out of trouble yet.

McKenzie and I would go round and round about eating at least once a week. Same conversation each time. I would ask her why she couldn't eat more and she would say she was eating plenty. I was usually pretty gentle but I would lose my cool at other times. As would she. She had an irritability that I had never seen before. I didn't know if it was because her body still might be starving or she was just protecting her behavior. Not willing to ever change. Or so it felt that way. Would we be stuck here forever? I never was willing to put up her cross country. In my heart I knew she would relapse. This was a chance I was not willing to take. She was having too much fun and feeling so good about herself. I to this day don't regret my decision.

So my plan next was to get her into another counselor that might do more things with her like trauma work. I did not feel she was making any progress with Ashley. So we found Cindy Hester. The counselor that would change my daughter's life.

Cindy had a way of making McKenzie feel like she was the most important person in the world. She helped McKenzie see that her emotions were important and needed to be appreciated not buried. McKenzie had no idea how to handle anxiety when she started out with Cindy. But by the time she was done, she had more ways to handle anxiety than I knew were available then. And McKenzie uses them to this day.

One race was run at a temperature of 103 degrees. I prayed the entire way there. 'God, please don't let my daughter die.' Apparently there had been a race a few years back where one of the schools lost a student due to the heat. Heat exhaustion is very very serious. It is caused by a loss of water and electrolytes. Symptoms are nausea, confusion, weakness, high body temperature, and irritability. It is a medical emergency. Once we got there, Mckenzie headed off to be with all the others. I usually had my partner or friend with me, but not this day. I headed off to the corner to have a meltdown. I had to watch her possibly die too many times. Was this going to be the day? I could have prevented her from running and I was questioning myself at this time. Did I make the wrong decision?

The girls lined up. The gun went off and off they went. I went running probably as fast as they did to the first point of observation. She was where she usually was in the pack. About a third of the way back. She liked to hang there awhile then move forward the last mile. She looked off but it was early.

Observation point number two, one mile, she was still a third back. Observation point three, she was starting to move forward. At this point, I was so proud of her I could have hugged everyone there. Now observation point four was the second mile. She was still moving forward. I tried to get a look of her face for any excessive sweating or strain from heat, but I couldn't tell.

Now we were heading for the end. As usual, McKenxzie was in the top ten. She was the only Shawnee Mission East girl up there. As they came around the last turn, I saw her face. She didn't look good. My heart sank. She was pale and very strained. I told her to stop, but I don't think she heard me. As they neared the end, girls were catching up. She was struggling. She finally made it to the finish. And so did I. She fell to the ground. Oh my God. She was in trouble. I ran up to her just when one of the coaches did too. Coach Pennington. Her favorite. McKenzie always felt like he cared. He practically carried her to a tent where they would put her on ice. When

I got to her she was slowed down in her responses but not so much confused. As she lay there, I had such fear. I had almost lost her before. Was this going to be it?

They hydrated her with some sort of electrolyte fluid and monitored her vitals. She was there for at least an hour while people were getting their stuff to leave. I held her hand the entire time. After an hour, she started to perk up.

She asked, "How did I do?"

I said, "Great!" I actually couldn't have cared less but she actually came into the top ten and qualified for state. That's my girl.

We made it through that day. But every race after that was a scary one. With time, my anxiety went down. But I would certainly never be quite the same. Races were dangerous and now I knew it.

The last two years at Shawnee Mission East were wonderful. She was making straight As and really enjoying school. She was one of the stars. They even had an article about her in the school newspaper.

Unfortunately, the eating wasn't changing. She continued to weigh in at 109 but behaviors were still there and I knew that was dangerous. At any time I felt like she could lose more weight and go back to the hospital. I stayed on her but without success. She continued to see Cindy. I noticed her outlook on life improving. She had a group of girls she ran around with and she just seemed happy.

Her senior year she became captain of the cross country team. It was an honor that made her stand a little taller. She also got into an honors program called the International Bachaleauate. It was a program that expected a lot more writing compared to the other classes. She excelled in school but she worked hard. There was running after school then three hours of homework. She seemed to love it but for some reason it didn't change her eating habits. She was hanging on to a piece of anorexia that needed to change but how?

Cross country continued to go well her senior year. She placed in the top ten in most of her races. We were thrilled. She was a long way from that little girl at the hospital with a tube down her throat.

Now was the time for making a decision on where she was going to go for college. McKenzie was excited. She felt with her grades she might do well. She also scored pretty high on the ACT: A thirty-eight. So she started applying but still not willing to gain weight staying at 108 to 109. I wanted her close by so I could watch her but I also wanted her to follow her dream.

CHAPTER 12

PAIN

"A man is what he thinks about all day long."

\- Ralph Waldo Emerson

So as I said McKenzie's academic performance was excellent. She applied to some of the most difficult schools to get into: Duke, University of Virginia, Stanford, and Emory. We were on pins and needles waiting for these school's responses. She loved Emory the most because it was a little smaller and according to the information McKenzie got it seemed more diverse. They recruit from a lot of Asian countries. It seemed like forever. Some other of her friends were getting into their school of choice. Shawnee Mission East has a very good reputation. Kids there get into Stanford, Harvard, Princeton, Yale and others. She finally got a no from Duke. Shoot. Nobody likes rejection but, she handled it well.

Two days later, she said she was staring at her computer in disbelief. She had gotten into Emory. Oh, it was so exciting. Atlanta, Georgia. Twelve hours away. Oh no. I was just starting to realize she was leaving. I was really starting to understand McKenzie. We were getting really close. So this is what it is like to give time to someone you love. It's a wonderful thing. I could tell she was starting to trust me more. She confided in me. So when she got into Emory I felt like I did too.

McKenzie left for Emory on August 10th, 2016. I drove her down. She took to it immediately. Of course, I cried all the way home. I was still so worried. We weren't out of the woods yet. She was still participating in her anorexia eating behaviors, only certain foods with limited portions. I saw her so happy for the next several months so why was she not eating well? It was hard because I couldn't watch her but I made a point to go down and see her as much as I could. I always weighed her when I saw her. Her weight was still holding at 109.

Here's where things get bad. McKenzie was home on spring break from her first year at college at Emory. She had called me at the office saying she was having severe abdominal pain. By the sound of her voice I knew it was very serious. Maybe it was my intuition. Either way, I immediately left my office and headed for home.

When I got there, she was rolling around the bed saying, "Mom, it hurts so bad."

I will never forget the look on my daughter's face. I knew this wasn't just constipation or gas, so I called 911. They were there in five minutes. Before I knew it she was on a stretcher heading for Saint Joseph Medical Center.

The ER at Saint Joseph was of course congested with all different kinds of things going on. Like an MI (heart attack), anaphylaxis, broken bones, and more. But luckily when you come in on a stretcher, you go to the front of the line. We found ourselves quickly in room 8. They helped McKenzie get on the bed as I stood right next to her holding her hand. What could be worse than watching your child in pain? She was rolling around on the bed pleading for help. I grabbed a nurse and said my daughter needs something for her pain, now! You don't mess around when it comes down to fighting for your kid. Momma bear came out.

Before you knew it, the doctor came in and ordered Dilaudid and an x-ray. Dilaudid gave her immediate relief. Of all the pain medications, Dilaudid is the second strongest after Fentanyl. It worked and she was finally able to talk. She told me the pain came out of nowhere. She said she had not changed her diet or medications. So why was she having this pain?

McKenzie was quickly wheeled out. I knew they were really concerned because things were going much faster than usual. She got back within twenty minutes and we just sat and waited for the doctor.

The doctor came in about twenty minutes later.

He had a severe look on his face and said, "McKenzie, you have a volvulus."

Oh my God, I knew this was not good. A volvulus is when a loop of intestine twists around on itself, resulting in a bowel obstruction. It can be so tightly twisted that blood stops flowing to that part of the intestine causing an is-chemic bowel. Not good. The intestine can rupture then sepsis. This can be caused by pregnancy, abdominal adhesions, constipation, and a high fiber diet. McKenzie fit the bill. Protein bars are high in fiber. Although I will say that protein bars definitely helped her maintain weight and provided some nour-ishment. The fiber in them can clog up your gut. This has to be it. The initial treatment for a volvulus is a sigmoidoscopy (when a tube is placed up the rectum into the large intestine for examination) after a barium enema. The doctor then will try to untwist the intestine then provide a clearing of the pipe, if you will. But patients frequently still need a bowel resection considering the high risk of recurrence. A gastroenterologist and general surgeon were both called in.

The general surgeon took me aside to tell me how serious this was and that she might not make it. Was this actually going to be McKenzie's last few days? I no longer just had numbness, I was in shock again. I couldn't breathe or move. Everything around me went into slow motion. I forgot where I was.

The doctor kept saying, "Dr. Willson, are you ok?"

Of course I wasn't, I was scared to death. I didn't have the time to get sup-port. I needed to be there for my daughter. I had to straighten myself up and take charge.

McKenzie was soon moved up to a bed in the hospital. She wasn't as scared for her life; she was more scared the pain would come back. And it did. Excruciating pain. I never heard someone have such a primal sound coming out of their mouth, but she couldn't articulate, she could only scream. She got Dilaudid every four hours. When it would wear off she would start screaming again. In all my years of practice I have never seen someone in this type of pain.

The night was long. I didn't sleep. I just held my daughter's hand and told her everything was going to be ok.

The next morning she was wheeled out first thing to see the gastroentero-logist (GI). I didn't know who to call so I called my mom. My mom is precious but her only way of dealing with something serious is to shut down. For ex-ample, when I was delivering McKenzie she was invited in with some of my friends. The labor was going on for hours to the point where the doctor was going to give me one more push and then it was C-section time. According to my friends, my mom closed her eyes and pretended to be asleep. So I wasn't so sure how she would react to all this but I gave it a try.

My mom answered after the first ring and said "What's up honey?"

I said, "Mom, McKenzie might die.

She quickly shot back, "Oh, she will be fine. What's wrong?"

She simply can't connect at these times. She couldn't be a better person but lived life by the philosophy that there is always a positive. This made her endure many things but as far as feeling the seriousness with me, she wasn't so good so I was feeling very alone and scared. I cried out in my head, "God, are you there?" I couldn't even cry, but I somehow was able to keep moving forward. I had no active support. Mostly because of me. I was too embarrassed to tell anyone. I didn't want to betray McKenzie because she asked me to not tell anyone. This moment in my life will never be forgotten. I will do my best to help others not to end up here.

All alone, McKenzie went down to see the gastroenterologist who was going to try and untwist some of her colon. This is called a colonoscopic decompression. A very difficult procedure.

I waited for at least four hours before she finally returned. Success! The doctor had skillfully decompressed the colon which now will allow the surgeon to go in and remove it. Because as I said before there is a high risk of this happening again. McKenzie still had pain but more manageable.

They planned on her having the surgery the next day. In the meantime, the GI doctor came up to check on McKenzie with his nurse. He was a very tall man, very clean shaven and wearing black horned rim glasses.

I stood up to give him a hug. I couldn't help it. He had saved my daughter's life. But I think he is on the spectrum, so that didn't go very well. He pulled back and acted very nervous.

His nurse quickly said, "Oh, let her hug you. You really helped her daughter."

He then came toward me still with his chart in front of him and tapped me on the back. Oh well. I could have hugged all day. We were halfway there. McKenzie and I spent the rest of the day talking about school.

McKenzie's surgery was planned for early the next morning. The surgeon came in and went over the procedure with us. I can't remember anything he said. I was way too scared. The next morning at 6 a.m., she was wheeled out.

I sat in her room for what seemed like forever. When she finally came back, the nurse said the surgery went very well. Her cecum was successfully removed and at this point there were no complications.

Even though I was so relieved I still felt on the ledge. The thought of her dying I am afraid, it took home in my brain. This was her third near death experience. Somehow I was able to keep going but I was definitely a little or a lot rattled. We stayed in the hospital for a few more days for observation then headed home.

Once home, we thought we were out of the woods, but the abdominal pain returned. Again, I called 911. As usual, they were there before I could get off the phone. We rushed to the hospital again. This time they took us to a closer hospital called Menorah. They wheeled McKenzie back right away just like before. This time they took her back for an x-ray, considering she just had surgery.

I waited in this room with McKenzie while she again was writhing in pain but not quite as bad as Saint Joseph. It was so difficult to just be an observer, waiting and praying for it to subside. For some reason they moved even faster than Saint Joseph in getting her an x-ray and the report came back quickly. McKenzie had a bowel obstruction. One of the complications of her surgery. So McKenzie was hospitalized again. She needed to stay there until her bowels moved. She was very uncomfortable. They had to put a tube down her to feed her again, but also to relieve pressure. It took a few days and a lot of pain but those bowels finally moved.

We had been on the edge of the cliff too many times. It was time to do something drastic. Neither she or I could go through another traumatic event. I was the mom I had to take control. So I got a plan.

CHAPTER 13

THE PLAN

"There is one thing which gives radiance to everything. It is the idea of something around the corner"

— G.K. Chesterton

So things had gotten too serious and McKenzie's eating behavior had to change. Her continued strict diet wasn't working. It seemed to be mostly protein bars. Her weight was still 109.

Emory had started back up again about the time McKenzie had her first surgery. So right after the first surgery, we wrote a letter to the dean to ask for special accommodations for her return to school. Usually they don't let you start late, but they were very generous with us. They approved it.

So once back home from her second surgery, we were getting McKenzie ready to go back when I started thinking I knew that McKenzie needed to change her behaviors and gain some weight. It was time to take more control.

McKenzie loved Emory, but of course I was paying for it. And it was expensive. I thought maybe it was time to use this as leverage. The best thing in McKenzie's life was Emory. She didn't even want to come home for breaks. It was a special school. There was a lot of diversity. McKenzie loved their philosophy of reaching out around the world to get students. Every day was a new experience for her. She loved her professors. It seemed all of them were so passionate about their area of study. Her major was neuroscience.

Was it time for me to give her an ultimatum where she couldn't continue at Emory unless she got into recovery? I needed another opinion.

I called my friend Madelyn who I knew had a good head on her shoulders. She also had compassion. She and I had lived together so she knew me well. This combination of things made her the friend to turn to. So I called.

"Madelyn, McKenzie has an eating disorder."

Madelyn had gone to several of McKenzie's meets so she knew about her weight problem, but not so much anorexia. I told her everything. I told Madelyn that she had improved but continues to have dangerous behavior. I told her I was thinking about not letting her go back to Emory without her getting more treatment and I meant it. What did she think?

I was scared to even say it out loud knowing how much it meant to her. Would it backfire? Not doing a program and actually coming home and getting worse. Was this going to be the worst decision I have ever made?

Madelyn came back with a very measured reply. She said it was time. Time for me to do something that mattered to her. That I was not a mean mother, I was a responsible one. I liked that word and hung on to it.

It was time to do a Rosie. Remember the young girl who was a basketball captain that got into recovery when she had to start eating or not play for the team? McKenzie had been weighing around 109-110 with a BMI of 18.1. We needed it higher. I had let her behaviors continue because she was eating enough to have a fairly satisfying weight, but I was rethinking this as I realized just how dangerous this borderline anorexic behavior could be. In our case it was all those protein bars.

After a long discussion with Madelyn on how to put this to McKenzie, noting that McKenzie was still dependent on me which could work in my favor. I got off the phone and called McKenzie. She had just been back to Emory for a few weeks. She answered the phone right away sounding very chipper. I thought, not for long.

Here's how it went.

"McKenzie, I have decided that you have to get into an eating recovery program and start eating more and different foods or you will have to leave Emory."

She screamed "No Mom!"

As I knew she would. I explained all the reasons why. I said, "It is likely that the volvulus was caused by your high fiber diet. Eating protein bars for a good part of your nourishment just isn't working. I know you eat a few other things but we are playing with fire. McKenzie, you still have anorexic behavior creating borderline malnourishment. For example, you avoid fat which is needed for your brain." I said to her that she was still teetering near the edge. Most importantly, she had not really changed her eating since she came out of the hospital when she was thirteen years old until now at age nineteen.

As I had said before, we would have many discussions about her diet that would usually end up in an argument. I felt helpless. Scared to be too forgiving but more scared to shame her. Shaming is the worst thing you can do to a child. I had been scared to do anything drastic for over six years since she was doing so much better than before the hospitalization. Some might say I should have done it earlier but I was afraid to put cross country on the line. She had been doing so well. She was so proud. But now I was more desperate. I was hoping she had enough identity from running and grades to let go. But soon found out it was more being an Emory student that made her the proudest.

McKenzie shot back all the reasons why she was ok. Like the fact she ate healthy meals (although not that much). She said she had been through counseling for three years and didn't need it anymore. She explained that if she did a program, her grades would be jeopardized. I didn't budge. Finally, she said she would think about it and hung up.

I got off the phone feeling very scared; couldn't move off the bed. I sat there with the phone in my hand for at least ten minutes. I called her back and left a message.

I said, "You need to let me know by tomorrow. I am hoping you will make the right decision. I have faith in you." And hung up, not knowing what she would do.

Not even an hour went by before she called back and said she would do it with a very angry voice. I told her she needed to get on it and find a treatment center for eating disorders. She said she would. I knew she didn't want to talk anymore, so we hung up. Here goes. I felt a little relieved.

CHAPTER 14

IDENTITY

"Self love is not so vile as self neglecting."
- William Shakespeare

There is importance for every child to have an identity but especially someone with possible anorexia or anorexia. Remember Erikson's levels of development. Remember identity versus role confusion. What do those terms really mean? It is an internal crisis. We need to know how to build identity? Many believe that your identity is found in early developmental years like seven to ten but the teen years have just as much influence. Think back to your teen years. Weren't kids labeled? Like the nerd, the jock, the teacher's pet, band geek, the photographer, the cheerleader, the artist, the religious freak, and more. These labels are given by your peers and they stick. The teen's peers will tell each other who they are. Sometimes good, sometimes not so good. But it sure helps if a parent can get in there with their child to figure it all out.

We need to encourage our children to explore things, trying things on to see what fits. I look at identity as two separate parts: values and skills. First values. What do they stand up for? Like not gossiping, being trustworthy, and honest. Treating their parents respectfully. Then skills. What are they good at?

Adolescence is a time where a child needs to be seen for their skills and talents. Recognized for their uniqueness, mostly by peers. Here are some things a teen can try: art, photography, journalism, debate, gardening, sports, cheerleading, band, theatre, leadership, politics, pep club, dance, drill team, woodwork, math, science, religion, and more. They might need encouragement and support while they try different things. They especially need support if they fail the first time which many people do fail on the first try of anything.

Then it's important to help them find their values. What do they stand up for? What do they want to have as a character quality? Values include perseverance, courage, compassion, fairness, equality, honesty, trustworthy, kindness, strength, and more. Give them role models to choose from who have stood for something and changed the course of time. For example, Rosa Parks sat on the bus, Abraham Lincoln stopped slavery, Eleanor Roosevelt brought literacy to the rural areas of the United States. Find examples in their school or in their activities. Look for teachers, coaches and other students that they can model.

The teen years are ripe for developing new behavior. The prefrontal cortex is the cortex in the brain that does executive functioning, decision making such as whether or not to eat ice cream when trying to lose weight and habits. This cortex controls impulses allowing the discipline of something to work. It also solves problems. So why is this important with identity? Well, if your teen starts developing good habits and skills, they are very likely to stick. For example, learning a language or a new sport. With practice, those neural pathways are laid down for life. Identity is shaped with practice. So important!

Also, the frontal lobe shrinks with malnourishment but returns to normal once nourished. Likely the shrinkage is the cause of irrational thinking and irritability.

CHAPTER 15

DECISIONS

"Life is the sum of all your choices."
- Albert Camus

I will never really know what all went on in my daughter's head the day she was forced into a decision. Treatment or no Emory. Somehow when forced to possibly lose something she loved she made the decision to get some help. I believe I was able to force her into a decision at this point, and not before, because now she had identity. Her identity was being a proud Emory student. The grades and running apparently weren't enough.

Emory was a very special school. It is a small school that is strong in both the sciences and the liberal arts. It has a diverse group of students from all over the world and it is small enough where the professors can get to know their students. And according to McKenzie, they were outstanding professors. There is nothing better than taking a class from a professor with a passion. McKenzie felt like she was at Harvard or better.

So McKenzie said she would research the area for a program. I don't think she was particularly planning on gaining weight but I made an expectation of her gaining two pounds as well, and more importantly, changing her eating habits to include more variety and more fat and carbo-hydrates.

McKenzie chose a program close to Emory that had a good reputation. The program was outstanding. She was in a night time class three days a week for three hours. They all ate dinner together.

McKenzie said she began to see she was not alone. She said, "Mom, they struggle with the same fears of losing control if they start eating."

They cried, sang, and prayed together. This got my daughter on the right course for the rest of her life. She finally knew she was not alone, and was feeling the fellowship. This is what it took at this particular time in her life.

Let's recap. We first want to catch possible anorexia before it gets traction. We do this by looking out for each other's kids and using the right words to say to a mom just like what Amy said to me. "Have you looked at your daughter lately?"

When identifying possible anorexia, get your medical team in place. Most important is a doctor who specializes in eating disorders. Additionally, you want to have a therapist and a nutritionist. Why not go all out and get all the support that is out there? Only you and your doctor can decide what level of care is appropriate, outpatient or inpatient. Remember there is no shame, just understanding. Next, start the family refeeding together. Have your child eat with you with as many meals as possible. This doesn't work for everyone but there is a high percentage of success. Finally, start helping your child with their identity, or we could also say competency. Find their skills and values. Skills and values can be found in or outside of the school. Such as churches, extended families, boy or girl scouts, and more. Make sure they feel seen and important. Make a big deal about whatever it is they are doing.

CHAPTER 16

TODAY

"Children have more need of models than of critics."

\- Carolyn Coats

I can't tell you how excited I am to introduce you to my daughter now. Please let our story give you hope. We had a tough road. There were some good and bad decisions but when it came down to it, McKenzie wanted life more than control. McKenzie finished Emory happy and healthy. She easily made her desired weight the rest of the time at Emory after she attended the out-patient program. She graduated with straight As with a major in neuroscience. After a year off, McKenzie got into the University of Kansas Medical School.

Mckenzie is now flourishing. Most important was she changed her eating habits. She still ate bars but not as much. She ate from all the food groups including dairy. After a month she had increased her weight found when weighing her to 115. You would be so proud of her. She runs almost every day or does a program called MoJo where she cycles with a group of others. But she can go for several days without running if too busy and be ok.

My daughter is the most wonderful person I know. She deeply cares about others, especially her mom. Right before writing this book I acquired a serious bout of pneumonia. We discovered this after a pickleball game where I was slurring my speech. My daughter went into doctor mode and recognized a problem immediately.

McKenzie came over and took me to the emergency room where they discovered I had pneumonia. My temperature was 101.7 and my O2 saturation was 89%. I went south quickly and had to be hospitalized. My daughter stood right by my side the whole time. She took two days off of school to take care of me.

As I looked at my daughter with her big brown eyes staring at me so compassionately and with such strength I thought, 'Boy, we have come a long way!'

CHAPTER 17

THE FUTURE

"The soul that has no established aim loses itself."

- George Hegel

Let me tell you how McKenzie lives now. Oh, how it has changed. First of all, and most importantly, she does not deny her emotions. She frequently calls me and says, "Mom, I am mad!" She used to not be able to identify what she was feeling. I am going to include in this book a "feelings chart" that has over a hundred different identified feelings. For example for anger there is agitated, annoyed, contempt, disappointed, discounted, enraged, frustrated, and so on. Make it a game at first until you and your child's feeling vocabulary picks up.

Let me give you an example of how McKenzie deals with a feeling. My mom is a very special woman but very stubborn when she wants something. There was a point last year where she insisted on McKenzie calling her cousins more often. This started to really annoy my daughter. So she told my mom she needed to decide on her own when she would call them. Instead of sitting in the "bad" feelings, she acted on them. Very important.

Another example is how McKenzie deals with the stress of med school by talking to me and her spin class buddies.

The next thing McKenzie does differently is she uses things available to her to nurse a difficult emotion. For example, she uses different songs by Taylor Swift that help her cheer up. For all you Taylor Swift fans, she loves "August".

In direct relationship to food, I will add that McKenzie doesn't skip meals. She eats all her meals around the same time and as I said it always includes dessert. She needs to eat a lot because she runs. And she does. She frequently has a peanut butter and jelly sandwich for breakfast, just like her mom.

I finally feel I have my feet on the ground again. It has been a long nine years with lots of terrifying moments. I only want to help parents catch anorexic behavior early to prevent more pain and have a much better chance at a good recovery.

McKenzie and I now have a wonderful relationship. A month ago we took a trip to Vancouver, Canada. We took hikes along the ocean watching the whales. Went to a large beautiful flower garden where we took pictures of each other with our favorite flowers and laughed the entire time.

McKenzie now calls me several times a week. We talk about everything. I think it would be safe to say that I am her "person". She and I have our silly shows we watch together. We try new and different restaurants together. She is doing so well in medical school. Plans on pursuing the field of pediatric neurology. Most importantly, as I said before, she loves to eat. You don't know how it feels to see her put away an ice cream sundae with a smile on her face. This is so much different than when all this started. I thought we were close but we really weren't. So this is truly a rainbow story.

CHAPTER 18

EATING DISORDER TYPES

"God helps the brave."
- J.C.F. von Schiller

Thus far we have thoroughly discussed anorexia nervosa. Here are all the eating disorders based on the Diagnostic and Statistical Manual of Mental Disorders (DSM-5).

I want to clarify something interesting. Individuals with restrictive eating might not be at a BMI less than 18.5 but might still be harming their body. They can be overweight and not get their nutrition so they have complications. For example, getting bilateral shin splints or a loss of their period. There is a known triad for girls malnourished; it consists of low bone mineral density, amenorrhea, and low energy.

Before we close I want to make you thoroughly understand anorexia nervosa. It can be of the restrictive type or the binge-eating/purging type. McKenzie, of course, had the restrictive type. The binge-eating/purging type has the same low body weight but there is binge/purging involved instead of restriction to get to the low body weight. I will talk about binge-eating and purging when I get to that disorder itself.

The next eating disorder is avoidant/restrictive food intake disorder different than anorexia. This is an eating disturbance manifested by persistent failure to meet appropriate nutritional or energy needs. For example, avoiding food based on sensory characteristics or fear of aversive consequences of eating necessary food. Not a fear of gaining weight. This is qualified by one of the following.

1. Significant weight loss.
2. Significant nutritional deficiency
3. Dependence on enteral feeding or oral nutritional supplements
4. Marked interference with psychosocial functioning
5. She was afraid of other food.

These individuals are frequently on the autism spectrum. For example, a thirteen-year-old child who since the age of six will only eat Chick Fil-A chicken nuggets for at least three months.

The next eating disorder is bulimia nervosa. This disorder is characterized by binge eating which is eating an amount of food definitely larger than what most individuals would eat with a sense of loss of control and inappropriate compensatory behaviors such as purging, laxative, diuretic or medication (levothyroxine), or exercise abuse.

Individuals that identify with this eating disorder are usually confused about relationship attachments. In the past they were thought of having confusion about their dependence on their mother this came along with some of Freud's ideas and have since been dismissed.

The next is just binge-eating disorder again characterized by eating a much larger amount than would be considered a normal amount of food within a two hour period. The binge episodes are associated with three of the following, at least once a week for three months paired with cross country.

1. Eating much more rapidly than normal.
2. Eating until feeling uncomfortably full.
3. Eating large amounts of food when not physically hungry.
4. Eating alone because you are embarrassed by how much one is eating.
5. Feeling disgusted with oneself with how much they ate.

The last thing I will talk about here is something called orthorexia. This is not listed in the DSM-5 but I think it is also important to identify. It is an obsession about eating proper or healthful eating becoming so fixated on it they lose their well-being. For example, they can only go to certain restaurants so when asked by friends to go to one not on their list they will decline and miss out on the fellowship.

Here are some warning signs of Orthorexia

1. Compulsive checking of ingredients lists and nutritional labels
2. An overly concern about the health of the ingredients
3. Only eating a narrow group of foods deemed healthy.
4. Spending hours a day thinking about what food might be served at an upcoming event.
5. Showing high levels of distress when "safe" foods aren't available.

My goal for this book is to help others identify early signs of eating disorders so as to direct the person toward a happier life. Let's all take responsibility for our community and save lives.

CHAPTER 19

LESSONS LEARNED

"A problem clearly stated is a problem half solved."

- Dorothea Brande

1. Carefully watch your child, as well as others for dysfunctional eating just like alcohol.

   Look for a thin child not eating, eating alone, or bizarre eating habits.

   If you notice signs of possible anorexia in someone else's child, don't be afraid to communicate with the parents. They need to know.

2. Once you identify possible anorexia in your child, get your team involved. A team should consist of a doctor and therapist who specializes in eating disorders, as well as a nutritionist.

3. Work with the doctor in deciding if your child needs hospitalization. Consider inpatient care if a BMI is less than 18.5.

4. Remember you do have a role in your child's success. Eat with them every possible meal. This is re-feeding using the Maudsley approach. You don't have to feel so helpless. They need to eat everything expected. Remember this has a high success rate.

5. Give your child a sense of identity by helping them pursue their values and skills. Especially pay attention to how they see themselves around their peers.

6. Identify any other comorbid issues such as depression, anxiety or bipolar. To have success these other problems need to be treated with either medication, therapy or both.

7. Be gentle but firm in your communication as you set boundaries or expectations. Again don't be afraid to be firm.
8. Give your child something to eat "for" like their love for basketball, Emory College, or any other dream.

The most important thing for you to do is to quickly obtain your own support system so you can be a stable force in your child's life. Something I didn't do until I finally called my friend.

My daughter is currently doing her pediatric rotation at Children's Mercy Hospital (CMH). Within the first week of the inpatient rotation the team admitted two young girls with eating disorders. I don't know all the details as that is kept private but I do know that both suffered from anorexia so I will tell you how impressed I am at CMH's protocol for a patient with anorexia.

First, they require bed rest so the patient doesn't burn more calories. Frequently patients will also be obsessed with exercise. The next thing they do is require the patient eat all of the three meals. Each meal must be eaten within thirty minutes. If the patient refuses to eat they get a nasogastric tube without discussion.

They are given a babysitter for twenty-four hours a day that prevents them from breaking the rules. There is observation in toileting and showering. No cell phone in order to prevent any social media disturbance. They are given a psychologist but not until a certain weight. At a low weight, the patient is unable to focus and process. CMH does not have a unit, they just provide the stabilization until the patient is transferred to an eating disorder program such as the Eating Recovery Center in Denver, Colorado.

Online support groups

1. Multi-Service Eating Disorders Association
2. ANAD support
3. ANAD mentoring
4. Project Heal
5. The Alliance for Eating Disorders Awareness
6. Recovery Record
7. Your Recovery Resource

Let's Save Lives!

Affectionate
Afraid
Agitated
Alarmed
Alone
Ambivalent
Angry
Annoyed
Anxious
Apathetic
Appreciated
Apprehensive
Ashamed
Attacked

Baffled
Betrayed
Blamed
Boiling
Bored
Brave

Calm
Caring
Cautious
Cleansed
Cold
Comforted
Compassionate
Concerned
Confident
Confused
Contempt
Controlled
Cooperative
Crazy
Crushed

Deceived
Defenseless
Defensive
Defiant
Demeaned
Depressed
Despair
Desparate
Determined

Dirty
Disappointed
Discounted
Discouraged
Disgusted
Disrespected
Distressed
Dread
Dissatisfied

Elated
Embarrassed
Empty
Encouraged
Enraged
Enthusiastic
Envious
Exasperated
Excited
Exhausted
Exposed

Fearful
Frustrated
Furious

Gloomy
Good
Grateful
Grieved
Guilty

Happy
Hassled
Hate
Helpless
Hopeful
Hopeless
Horrified
Hostile
Humiliated
Hurt
Hysterical

Ignored
Impatient
Important

Impressed
Inadequate
Insecure
Irritated
Isolated
Intimidated

Jealous
Joy

Leery
Left out
Lonely
Lost
Love
Loved
Loving
Lust

Mad
Manipulated
Miserable
Misunderstood

Needed
Neglected
Nervous
Nostalgic
Numb

Overwhelmed
Ostracized

Pain
Panic
Patient
Peaceful
Playful
Pleasure
Proud
Pushed away

Reassured
Rebellious
Regretful
Rejected
Relaxed

Relieved
Remorseful
Resentful
Ridiculed

Sad
Safe
Satisfied
Scared
Secure
Sensitive
Sexual
Shocked
Shook up
Shy
Sick
Silly
Smothered
Special
Supported
Surprised
Suspicious
Sympathetic

Taken advantage
Tense
Terrified
Thankful
Timid
Torn
Trapped

Unappreciated
Uncertain
Uncomfortable
Unease
Unhappy
Unimportant
Unloved
Unprotected
Unsafe
Unsure
Used

Warm
Worried
Worthless

Jane Head M.A., 7133 W. 95th St., Overland Park, KS 66212, 913 649-9200

www.ingramcontent.com/pod-product-compliance
Lightning Source LLC
Chambersburg PA
CBHW061351140726
47997CB00003B/1160